The Engagement Manifesto

The Engagement Manifesto

A SYSTEMIC APPROACH
TO ORGANISATIONAL SUCCESS

R ALAN CROZIER

authorHOUSE®

AuthorHouse™
1663 Liberty Drive
Bloomington, IN 47403
www.authorhouse.com
Phone: 1-800-839-8640

First published by AuthorHouse   07/25/2011

ISBN: 978-1-4567-8573-4 (sc)
ISBN: 978-1-4567-8574-1 (hc)
ISBN: 978-1-4567-8575-8 (ebk)

CONTENTS

For Rod, Jamie and Grant.

You knew I would leave you something . . .

INTRODUCTION

"There are men with bold ideas, but highly critical of their own ideas; they try to find whether they are not perhaps wrong. They work with bold conjectures and severe attempts at refuting their own conjectures."—Sir Karl Popper (1902-1994)

In 1996 I had an idea for a book. This isn't it, but much of the philosophical underpinning is the same. The difference is in the focus, and hopefully because of the time lapse (partly due to the sentiment expressed above), as well as 14 years of hypothesising, testing, and practice, the product is the better for it.

While the title and much of the focus of this book is about employee engagement, trying to understand it and creating the environment to nurture it, that is not the overarching purpose. The real objective is better and sustainable organisational performance. That is the destination; employee engagement is the route map.

This book should be read by any senior manager, but it will have particular significance for CEOs, human resource practitioners and those responsible for organisational communication. It will hopefully also be of use to students or those starting out in their careers. The aim is to catalyse a re-examination of what you are doing in the name of engagement.

For longer than I care to remember, annual reports have stated that employees are the organisation's greatest asset, but more often than not, the behaviours exhibited by these organisations do not reflect that sentiment. There has been a significant change; "people" are now further up the corporate agenda—and for good reason. This gave rise to people-focused initiatives and an increase in organisational specialisms: total rewards, learning and development, communication management, and more recently, employee engagement.

As soon as a concept is given a label, it is in danger of being misinterpreted and executed badly. It is then in danger of being dismissed as the latest fad. I worry about that for engagement. I have seen companies doing surveys that measure satisfaction and calling them engagement surveys. I have seen three published surveys in the past two years that were called engagement surveys but that only measured communication effectiveness. We will see how satisfaction and engagement are different in their antecedents and outcomes, and that communication, while vital and omnipresent, is not omniscient in this process.

What follows is a pragmatic view of employee engagement and its contribution to organisational performance. It is based on developing and testing a hypothesis, practicing the principles with organisations, and testing employee and employer opinion on what works for them. It is hopefully a practical process that can be started at any given point and followed through to drive real benefits for an organisation. This is a mixture of theory, practice, research and experience; it is not intended to be an academic treatise. If the academics own the classical version, this is the blues/rock version, which provides the overarching chord structure for you to add the melody.

Engagement deserves more status and greater respect than it currently enjoys. It has to occupy the right space in the organisational psyche. We will look at the context in which we have to consider employee engagement: core purpose, values, and culture; try to get some clarity on what it means; and how you can influence it, measure it, and most important, drive performance through your people. Consider it your new manifesto.

Alan Crozier, Glasgow, May 2011

1. SEARCHING FOR THE SILVER BULLET

There was a time when, if you "kept your nose clean," you could have a job for life. If you were loyal, worked hard, and did as you were told, your employer would provide a job, award regular pay increases, and provide a degree of financial security—even in retirement. Problems arose when the pace of change accelerated. New players from emerging economies entered the market, competition became much stiffer, the rules of the game changed and traditional companies struggled with the speed of this process.

What followed was a period of "re-engineering" in which businesses were restructured, refocused, down-sized (or right-sized), and people were expected to "work smarter not harder." Those who were not laid off were expected to stay, follow orders and do at least part of someone else's job as well as their own. In return, their employer would provide employment (while they could) and pay them the same as before but make gestures that they cared about them as employees. Perhaps not surprisingly with hindsight, people did not always stay with their employers simply because they at least had a job. They started to look for ways to take charge of their careers and sought out better opportunities and better employers. Companies that did not come to terms with this new reality haemorrhaged talent.

The employer-employee relationship has now evolved from the parent-child state described in the first paragraph to an adult-adult state in which the new employment deal is more of a strategic partnership. Companies expect their people to develop the skills that they need and apply them in ways that help the business, meanwhile displaying behavioural competencies consistent with those of the company.

In return, they will provide challenging work, support professional development, reward individual contribution and treat people like adults.

In most advanced economies, regardless of the unemployment statistics, there is a skills shortage of some sort. Recognising that people generally, but key talent particularly, are core drivers of value, organisations have to develop the ability to attract, fully engage and retain that talent.

Around the time competition for talent was on the rise, the phrase "employer of choice" emerged. This struck a chord with many companies, and it became a popular strap line (or tag line) in recruitment materials as companies sought to differentiate themselves in the market. While the meaning of the phrase is immediately understood, what it means in practice is less clear. To many companies, it means simply being flexible with total reward or being creative with professional development opportunities. What is clear was that the currency and effectiveness of the strap line decreases in inverse proportion to its popularity. It is not effective enough to say, "We are an employer of choice"; companies have to *be* an employer of choice without stating it. This requires a more robust and holistic approach.

Companies have always sought to find and exploit an advantage over the competition. Price, quality, speed, effectiveness, and fitness for purpose are the traditional battlegrounds in the war to attract and retain business. As organisations pursue their holy grail, however that is expressed, they are often tempted by what some would call management fads. There is an overwhelming desire to find the silver bullet that will make all the difference. Initiatives become fashionable and in the process highly visible. Total Quality Management; Just in Time procurement; Six Sigma; 100 Best Companies to work for; the Learning Organisation; Balanced Scorecard; and many more.

These initiatives are laudable, practical and effective in their own way, but as more organisations adopt them; and as the timescale from innovation to imitation is measured in weeks rather than years, and anyone can buy the latest IT infrastructure, production process or marketing campaign; competitive advantage is harder to find and even harder to hold onto.

The foregoing initiatives simply allow companies to be *in* the game, but what do they need to do to *win* in that game?

Drivers of capital

When looking at the value of a business, we have to consider a number of things.

First, there are physical assets: land, buildings, plant and machinery, stock. Physical capital if you like. Then consider the company's ability to raise money, leverage its assets, and meet its financial obligations: financial capital. Taken together, this represents the value of the organisation's tangible assets.

We also have to consider the knowledge, competencies and relationships in the business that can be used to create differential advantage. We used to refer to at least the relationships part as "goodwill"; now we call the whole intellectual capital. Adding all three components together gives us an indication of the market value of the enterprise.

The ratio of market value to replacement cost of assets is known as Tobin's Q.

This ratio was devised by James Tobin of Yale University, Nobel laureate in economics, who hypothesised that the combined market value of all the companies on the stock market should be about equal to their replacement costs. (http://moneyterms.co.uk/tobins-q/). The Q ratio is calculated as the market value of a company divided by the replacement value of its assets. A low Q (between 0 and 1) means that the cost to replace a firm's assets is greater than the value of its shares. This implies that the share price is undervalued. Conversely, a high Q (greater than 1) means that a firm's shares are more expensive than the replacement cost of its assets, which implies that the shares are overvalued. This measure of share valuation is the driving factor behind investment decisions in Tobin's model.

When one company buys another for a premium over the share price, it is usually because they see additional value in synergies and the organisation's intellectual capital, which has three components:

1. Customer capital: the value of the organisation's sales and customer relationships
2. Structural capital: the ability of the organisation to capture, manage, and replicate its knowledge and competencies
3. Human capital: the value of the knowledge, competencies, expertise, experience and disposition of its employees. (Used in its proper context, human capital is not a synonym for human resources, personnel or indeed people.)

What is significant is that in most of today's organisations, operating as they do in a knowledge economy, the value of intellectual capital outstrips the value of the tangible assets by quite a margin. More important, when you examine the intellectual capital construct, it is totally dependent on human intervention.

But it wasn't always viewed this way.

Does history repeat itself?

Maybe not precisely, but there are some recurring themes (Fig. 1.1)

Management thinking

Date	Philosophy	Date	Philosophy
1900 - 1930	Taylorism 'One right way'	1970 - 1990	IT Revolution Automate/control (neo-Taylorism)
1930 - 1936	Classical Administration Organise by: function; geography; line of business	1990 - 1995	Business Process Re-engineering 'Don't automate, obliterate' (neo-classical administration)
1950 - 1970	Human Resources The rise of the 'personnel' practitioner	1995 -	A growing appreciation of people as a value-driver (human capital); and **The Engagement Manifesto**

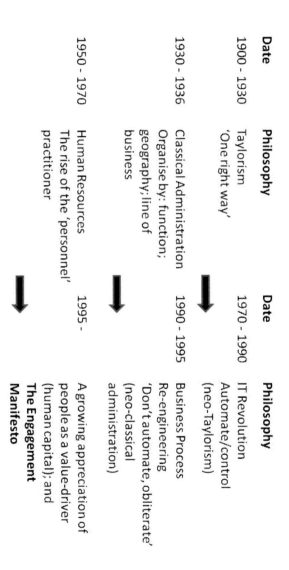

Fig 1.1

Frederick Winslow Taylor (1856-1915), widely known as F. W. Taylor, was an American mechanical engineer who sought to improve industrial efficiency. He is regarded as the father of scientific management and was one of the first management consultants. Taylor thought that by analysing work, 'one best way' could be found to perform tasks. He is probably best remembered for developing the time and motion study.

Workers were supposed to be incapable of understanding what they were doing. According to Taylor this was true even for rather simple tasks.

"I can say, without the slightest hesitation," Taylor told a congressional committee, "that the science of handling pig-iron is so great that the man who is physically able to handle pig-iron and is sufficiently phlegmatic and stupid to choose this for his occupation is rarely able to comprehend the science of handling pig-iron". (Montgomery, David (1989), *The Fall of the House of Labor: The Workplace, the State, and American Labor Activism, 1865-1925*, Cambridge University Press)

We may find that amusing now but before you laugh, read on. From the early 1970s an IT revolution was unfolding that would enable us to automate and control much of what happens in the workplace and now of course even in the home—or when we are mobile. Isn't this a form of neo-Taylorism?

In the 1930s businesses started to think more about the ways in which they were structured and we had a period of what was called classical administration. Companies would organise by function, by geography, or by line of business for example. Sixty years later in 1990, Michael Hammer, a former professor of computer science at the Massachusetts Institute of Technology (MIT), published an article in the *Harvard Business Review*, in which he claimed that the major challenge for managers is to obliterate non-value adding work, rather than using technology for automating it. http://hbr.org/1990/07/reengineering-work/ar/1

Business Process Reengineering (BPR), the concept of reviewing organisational processes was adopted by many organisations and became a major source of revenue for consulting firms. It was seen as a new tool for achieving business success and much space in journals and books was dedicated to it. Critics however claimed that it increased managerial control, de-humanised the workplace and started a downsizing frenzy. Neo-classical administration? Not all BPR exercises delivered on their early promise largely because their architects forgot, or more likely failed to consider that it is people who make change happen.

Talking of people; from the 1950s employees were beginning to be given slightly more consideration in the workplace. Welfare officers were appointed to look after employee wellbeing occasioned by service personnel returning to work after the Second World War. The Welfare people were frequently retired Commissioned Officers. In parallel with this Work Study started to take off, estimating the time taken for specific tasks and rewarding employees on volume completed (piecework). Taylorism at work. As more regulation was introduced to the workplace by government to protect workers

(e. g. health and safety legislation); the unions found support in their cause for looking after workers interests. Also at this time, businesses were starting to realise that people weren't just pairs of hands; they had skills and competencies and had to be fit for purpose. A more robust form of recruitment and selection was needed and all of these people issues were incorporated in to the Personnel Department.

By the late sixties and into the mid-eighties the unions became so strong that the major players in the 'personnel' arena were the Industrial Relations Managers (nowadays more likely referred to as Employee Relations Managers). The unions driven by their own agenda were generally the adversaries of management.

Fast forward to today, and *people* are firmly back on the agenda. The unions see themselves as part of the solution rather than always playing an adversarial role.

The personnel department has become the Human Resources function, or the People function and it has become more sophisticated encompassing varying and related disciplines with their own nomenclature: reward (compensation and benefits); learning and development; training; talent management; succession planning; and very often, employee communication; there are probably others.

Adding value

Despite this growth in sophistication and numbers, the HR function has been slow to quantify its impact on the organisation. It can talk about head count, staff turnover, absenteeism, accident rates, and recruitment costs; but how does the function seek to measure its strategic impact? Is it because it is seen as too difficult? This lack of promotion of the strategic value that HR adds to the enterprise allows other senior executives to continue to believe that it is a business cost rather than a value-driver.

There are published studies (e g Watson Wyatt's Human Capital Index™) which clearly show where good HR practice adds value and by regression analysis identifies the components that add most value. That may differ from company to company but HR seems in many cases constrained to managing process, ticking the correct boxes ensuring that it is compliant rather than helping to develop and drive strategy. Despite HR being responsible for the people strategy ('our greatest asset') there are comparatively few practitioners with a seat at the top table. What can operations, finance or marketing do without the influence of people? Could an engagement philosophy provide the impetus for HR including internal communication to move from internal consultant to strategic partner?

The hard-nosed business executive might argue then that human capital is an asset to be leveraged. But you know better; we're dealing with people, and they have to be engaged.

There is no silver bullet, but there is an arsenal.

2. DECONSTRUCTING ENGAGEMENT

The biggest problem with engagement is that everyone thinks they know what it means, but they use the same word to describe different constructs, all of which purport to enhance business performance in some way. Here we will examine these different constructs and hopefully end up with a workable definition and practical tool set to further our consideration of the antecedents of engagement and their potential consequences.

First though, we have to consider the journey in contemporary thinking. For many years job satisfaction was considered nirvana and a determinant of organisational performance. Then someone decided that job involvement was the real driver. Hold that thought—no, maybe it's organisational commitment? This subsequently became known as organisational citizenship behaviour (OCB; individual discretionary behaviour, Robinson et al 2004). Added to that even now there are those who claim to have found a silver bullet.

A populist perspective

Early in 2010, an article appeared in the business section of *The Sunday Times* entitled, "You just need love to make a profit." The subject of the article was an interview with Cleve Stevens, a California-based consultant whose mission in life is convincing business leaders that caring for their people will help them drive bottom-line benefits. The article didn't go into the detail of the approach, but it seemed to be based on transformational leadership (an approach which enhances the motivation, morale and performance of individuals aligned to organisational goals and values). He cited the case of Cox Arizona, which attributed massive business growth to this approach.

Logically, leadership will be a critical component in any engagement construct, but one must question whether transformational leadership on its own can sustain stellar performance. Mustn't there be something else supporting it?

HCL Technologies is one of India's largest companies, with revenues of £1.8 billion and a worldwide employee population of 55,000. Its Vice Chairman and CEO Vineet Nayar eschews the deference accorded to CEOs and has a management philosophy of employee focus. "Employee First, Customer Second" is his mantra, and it is based on the following principle: Happy employees mean happy customers. The moments of truth for the business are at the customer-employee interface, and this is where value is created.

It is difficult to argue with this notion, but Nayar's focus seems to be predicated on employee satisfaction driven largely by open communication. However, as the following example demonstrates, employee satisfaction does not equal employee engagement. Employees at one of the oldest banks in the U.K. stated in annual surveys that they were satisfied with their jobs, very satisfied with their employer and would recommend the company to others as a place to work. But the bank was underperforming its sector.

A closer look at the employer-employee relationship revealed the source of the disconnection. People were paid in line with the market and received a bonus every Christmas regardless of their personal performance. They enjoyed a non-contributory final salary pension scheme; they were able to benefit from cheap loans and discounted mortgages; they had recently introduced a flexible benefits programme; and, significantly, the bank rewarded tenure rather than performance when it came to pay raises and promotions, with a guaranteed no redundancy policy.

Of course people were satisfied, but they weren't performing. They were too comfortable. The bank's people policies were paternalistic; they hadn't even considered the engagement imperative, and they paid a heavy price. Within 18 months, they were taken over by another bank. Advocacy therefore does not necessarily mean engagement.

A Government perspective

The U.K. government under the Brown Labour administration took a keen interest in employee engagement. David MacLeod and Nita Clarke were asked by the then Secretary of State for Business in late 2008 to take an in-depth look at employee engagement and to report on its potential benefits for companies, organisations and individual employees. When the new Secretary of State, Lord Mandelson, met them earlier that year as the recession was worsening, he encouraged them to examine in particular whether a wider take-up of engagement approaches could positively impact U.K. competitiveness and performance as part of the country's efforts to come through the current economic difficulties, take maximum advantage of the upturn when it arrived, and meet the challenges of increased global competition.

In their report, "Engaging for Success: Enhancing Performance through Employee Engagement" (2009), their answer is an unequivocal yes:

> In the course of the past eight months we have seen many examples of companies and organisations where performance and profitability have been transformed by employee engagement; we have met many employees who are only too keen to explain how their working lives have been transformed; and we have read many studies which show a clear correlation between engagement and performance—and most importantly between improving engagement and improving performance.

(MacLeod, D. & Clarke, N. *Engaging for Success: enhancing performance through employee engagement 2009, Introduction p.3).*

The report does not propose that this should be remedied by a top-down, heavy-handed government intervention as MacLeod explains: "In our view extending employee engagement is not an issue for legislation or regulation: it requires culture change. More people need to 'get it'—and more people need to do it." (p. 6)

In a paper prepared specifically for the Macleod Review (2009), David Guest, professor of organisational psychology and human resource management at Kings College London suggested that, "… the concept of employee engagement needs to be more clearly defined [. . .] or it needs to be abandoned" (p. 8).

Some have suggested that engagement is nothing more than "old wine in a new bottle," but the MacLeod Review concluded that there was too much momentum and excellent work being done in the name of employee engagement for its abandonment: "Engagement is about establishing mutual respect in the workplace for what people can do and be, given the right context, which serves us all, as individual employees, as companies and organisations and as consumers of public services. It is our firm belief that it can be a triple win: for the individual at work, the enterprise or service, and for the country as a whole." (p. 6)

The government endorsed the views of MacLeod and agreed to develop its approach to engagement further and find ways to support business in that endeavour. At the time of writing, the new coalition government has announced that it is to set up a task force headed by MacLeod to take this initiative forward. It recognises that as we struggle to come out of recession, an engaged workforce is a necessity.

An academic perspective

Academics writing on the subject of engagement seem happy to start with the premise that engagement is a desired state and that there are direct benefits accruing to the employer organisation. Their focus is on trying to establish the unique nature of engagement as compared to other constructs and, more precisely, to describe what that might be and how it is manifested.

Engagement typically refers to a psychological state. We attach other descriptors by way of explanation: involvement, initiative, commitment. It usually connotes some form of volition or energy, which is described both attitudinally and behaviourally. Engagement is ". . . an amalgamation of commitment, loyalty, productivity, and ownership" (Wellins & Concelman, 2005, p.1)

In their paper, "The Meaning of Employee Engagement" Macey and Schneider (2006) offer three facets of engagement: trait engagement, state engagement and behavioural engagement. Trait relates to the characteristics of a person, who may have positive views of life and work and be proactive, altruistic and conscientious by nature. State refers to feelings about the job role; the energy and absorption of the person in that role; and their involvement, satisfaction, commitment and empowerment. Behavioural engagement manifests as extra-role behaviour. An example would be organisational citizenship behaviour (OCB) taking the initiative, doing more than the role demands, and displaying adaptive behaviours.

Macey and Schneider (2006) further posit that the nature of work itself has a direct impact on state engagement and can moderate the relationship between trait and state. Leadership has a direct impact on state engagement and trust, and through trust, an indirect impact on behaviour. Trust in leadership, therefore, has a direct impact on behavioural engagement.

According to "Work 2000," a study by Watson Wyatt Worldwide, the drivers of trust are:

- Explaining reasons behind major decisions.
- Gaining support for the business direction.
- Promoting the most qualified employees.
- Motivating employees to perform.
- Acting on employee suggestions.

- Providing job security.
- Encouraging employee involvement.

Writing well in advance of most academics on this subject, Kahn (1990) stated,

"People can use varying degrees of their selves, physically, cognitively, and emotionally, in the roles they perform—the more people draw on their selves to perform their roles—the more stirring are their performances" (p. 692-724).

In his 2006 paper, Saks cites Maslach et al (2001) stating that engagement is characterized by energy, involvement and efficacy—the direct opposite of the three burnout dimensions of exhaustion, cynicism and inefficacy. Research on burnout and engagement found that the key characteristics of burnout—exhaustion and cynicism—and engagement—vigour and dedication—are polar opposites (Gonzales-Roma et al, 2006). Further, Maslach et al (2001) identified six moderators of the burnout/ engagement scale:

1. Workload
2. Control
3. Reward and recognition
4. Community and social support
5. Perceived fairness
6. Values

Workload has to be balanced and sustainable. People want to feel that they have some control and choice in their work. Reward and recognition should be appropriate, colleagues should be supportive, policies and processes should be fair in their design and execution, and employees need to feel that their contributions are worthwhile and valued.

The foregoing helps to explain the environment that may lead to engagement, but it doesn't explain how or why people might respond by becoming engaged. Saks argues that lies in Social Exchange Theory (SET), which points to a symbiotic relationship between employer and employee, a mutual interdependence.

A basic tenet of SET is that relationships evolve over time into trusting and mutual commitments as long as each side keeps to the "bargain." That bargain usually means the actions by one party lead to a response by the other. Therefore, when people receive economic or socio-emotional resources from their organisation, they feel obliged to reciprocate and repay the organisation (Cropanzano & Mitchell, 2005).

Some may question whether people are engaged with their job or with their organisation. The preferable state is for them to be engaged with both. That is what will lead to positive consequences.

Much confusion arises because, to some people, job satisfaction or satisfaction with the employer and engagement are directly linked. Some surveys have confused this issue. Harter et al (2002) described the Gallup Work Place Audit as "satisfaction-engagement." The issues being assessed relate to working conditions and cognition rather than to the affective state. In other words, this tool measures satisfaction rather than engagement. The latter would require an assessment of such attributes as involvement, commitment and enthusiasm.

Engagement therefore is much more than satisfaction in that people have to give of themselves in an engaged state. While there is room for satisfaction within the engagement construct, engagement connotes activation, whereas satisfaction connotes satiation (Erikson, 2005). It would appear then that people can be satisfied and not remotely engaged; however, it is difficult to imagine a situation in which employees are engaged but not satisfied.

Based on the foregoing, we can begin to construct a picture of the antecedents of engagement: leadership, trust, choice, control, characteristics of the job, reward, involvement, empowerment, fairness as well as the characteristics of people.

The practitioner's perspective

It is an unfortunate fact of life that practitioners, whether in-house or in consulting, don't have the luxury of doing the reading or research necessary to form a forensic view of engagement. They are working on projects, adhering to deadlines and largely playing what's in front of them. They've been doing that for years and have developed a view of engagement from their own perspective, experience and discipline. As we have discussed, until comparatively recently, this issue has been championed and driven solely by those in the field. It is no surprise then that there are probably as many definitions of engagement as there are practitioners.

Depending on where you look, engagement has been defined as anything from satisfaction to discretionary effort to advocacy. We have seen that satisfaction is not the answer and discretionary effort as a measure is questionable if not properly directed. Advocacy on its own could not be confidently stated as a sign of engagement, we would have to find other supporting evidence. If engagement is to drive organisational performance, there has to be a strong line-of-sight to organisational objectives as well as the concomitant dedication to help achieve them.

For the purposes of this discussion and the ensuing chapters, here's a pragmatic definition in two parts from this practitioner's viewpoint, one concerned with employees, the other with the engagement process:

1. Engaged employees are those who are cognitively, attitudinally, and behaviourally aligned with and committed to their job role and their organisation's objectives.
2. Employee engagement is the ongoing process of creating the environment in which the values, systems, policies, and behaviours adopted by the organisation are congruent with and supportive of the pursuit of its objectives through its people.

There are inherent critical dependencies in these definitions if enhanced organisational performance is the objective. We'll look at those in more detail in Chapter 5.

For the moment, hold these thoughts:

- Employee engagement requires systemic rather than reductionist thinking
- Employee engagement is a process, not an event
- Employee engagement is a way of doing business, not an intervention
- Employee engagement is the journey, not the destination
- Employee engagement can be fragile; it is not a permanent state

Now let's consider the environment and context that condition engagement.

3. INTRODUCING THE THREE TENETS

When considering business strategies, the Japanese recommend looking at the issue from the perspective of the hawk and the ant: the hawk for the big picture, the ant for the detail. You can look through the eyes of the ant in your own organisational context; but for the hawk's perspective, this writer has three tenets that form the overarching principles guiding performance through engagement:

1. The company doesn't exist.
2. Organisations are dynamically complex adaptive systems.
3. Employees are a dynamic asset.

Let's deal with those in turn.

The company doesn't exist

"Of course it exists," you might say, "it's a legal entity. Look at the factory, the offices, the branding!"

Company comes from the Latin *com panis*, which literally means "with bread," and so we can imagine people breaking bread together. Company, therefore, has come to mean an assembly of people, a society. In the context of the formal construct, it means people working together for a common purpose or goal. The point here is that without people (no matter whether it is one person or 100,000) nothing happens; the company doesn't exist.

The diagram (Fig 3.1) shows how companies (or other human organisations) are constructed by people and have to work through people to achieve their purpose. On the left side of the model, we can see how some people in the organisation, "the bosses," decide on their vision of the future for the enterprise and their mission or core purpose. There is a set of core values to guide them, and they adopt various strategies and tactics to achieve their aims.

R Alan Crozier

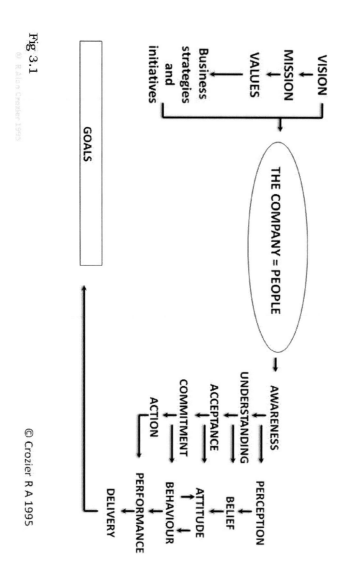

THE COMPANY DOESN'T EXIST

VISION → MISSION → VALUES → Business strategies and initiatives

THE COMPANY = PEOPLE

AWARENESS → PERCEPTION
UNDERSTANDING → BELIEF
ACCEPTANCE → ATTITUDE
COMMITMENT → BEHAVIOUR
ACTION → PERFORMANCE
→ DELIVERY

GOALS

Fig 3.1
© R Alan Crozier 1995

© Crozier R A 1995

What is significant then, is that there is no direct link between establishing their goals and aspirations and achieving them. For that they have to work through another set of people, "the staff." In so doing, they must ensure that the staff is aware of what they are trying to do, understand it, buy in to it and get on with it in a consistent fashion.

That seems simple enough, but the staff isn't an amorphous mass of automatons who will simply comply. They are people who bring their own belief systems to work, have preconceptions about the world and everything in it, and attitudes to go with them. The bosses have to be able to comprehend and tap into the psyche of various groups or individuals to ensure trust so that their influence can condition organisational beliefs and attitudes, which encourages the appropriate behaviours. Sometimes people will act in the desired way despite their attitude, maybe swayed by reward, for example. Over time and by habit, behaviour can change attitude, which of course reinforces the desired behaviour. When people perform their required tasks with the right frequency and intensity, performance meets objectives. The bosses are happy and probably get a bonus. Whether the staff is engaged is another matter.

Organisations are dynamically complex adaptive systems

The earth is part of the solar system. The earth also has systems: an ecosystem, a weather system, etc. The country in which you live is a system and has its own systems: a political system, a legislative system, a transportation system and so on. Your home has an electrical system, a heating system, a water system. You are a system with subsystems: a digestive system, a nervous system, a brain, a reproductive system, a vascular system. The organisation in which you work is a system. We are both surrounded by and part of many systems.

A system is an entity that maintains its existence and functions as a whole through the interaction of its parts. (O'Connor & McDermott 1997).

Some systems are simple, like a thermostat on your heating system. It switches on below a certain temperature and off again when it reaches a pre-set desired temperature. Some systems can be complex in detail, like a computer. When everything is properly connected, the software installed and commands given in the right order, it can produce wondrous things. But an illicit intrusion, a power spike or the wrong sequence of commands can render it useless.

There are systems that are both complex and dynamic. Whereas the computer is complex in detail—there is one way that it all connects to produce results—the system that is dynamically complex has parts that can assume different states and can be connected in different ways. The number of parts is irrelevant; the degree of dynamic complexity is what makes the system's behaviour harder to predict.

The organisation in which you work is a dynamically complex adaptive system. It is constantly changing, but it still persists. It has the capacity to change and learn from experience. Systems have laws, of which we should be aware, as these may guide our understanding and actions. Systems have emergent properties that cannot be found in their parts. These properties are only recognizable when the system is working; therefore, deconstructing the system into its components won't tell us what it will be like when it is working.

Imagine that you had never seen or heard an orchestra but that you had access to the individual instruments and the musicians. You could hear them being played expertly, but nothing could prepare you for the experience of hearing them play together as an orchestra. Imagine what it would be like, having seen and heard the components, then to experience the emergent property. Breaking the orchestra down into pieces won't reveal the sound, and cutting it in half won't give you two orchestras but two dysfunctional bands.

Analysis is useful for looking at how complex systems might fit together but not to determine how they might work. To do that, we have to put the system together in a careful, synergistic and congruent way, and then look for the emergent properties.

When working in a system, you can never do just one thing. Systems thrive on feedback loops. And feedback will be one of two kinds: reinforcing or balancing. Systems have their own volition and are particularly adept at sustaining themselves.

However if an intervention is considered bad for the system, and the feedback is reinforcing, the consequences could be disastrous. If good coupled with reinforcing feedback, the outcome is likely to be more positive. A good intervention witnessing balancing feedback may die in its infancy, and a bad one may never see the light of day. But it's not quite that simple because there isn't always a direct link between cause and effect; they are not limited in time and space, and the effect becomes the cause for yet another effect.

Politicians are particularly bad at cause and effect. If we do x, y will happen—completely ignoring the fact that they are operating in and with systems. For example, since tobacco is bad for people's health, politicians decide to tax it, raising the price to encourage people to stop (and incidentally increasing revenues). Maybe a few people will stop, but tobacco theft and smuggling have also become lucrative criminal activities, not just because the politicians created a margin to be earned, but because the penalties are less severe than those for drug-dealing. This demonstrates another law of systems: Expect side effects. Young people take up smoking because it is "cool," and their peers are doing it; they're not interested in health issues because they think these don't apply to them. If politicians were thinking systemically, they would look for ways to galvanize non-smoking teenagers to come up with something "cooler" than smoking.

An effect isn't necessarily in proportion to its cause. "Does the flap of a butterfly's wings in Brazil set off a tornado in Texas?" That was the subject of a paper delivered by meteorologist Edward Lorenz at Massachusetts Institute of Technology (O'Connor, J., & McDermott, I., The Art of Systems Thinking, *Thorsons 1997*, p. 88). He found that small variations in calculations of weather patterns would produce completely different weather systems over time. This links to the concept of leverage in systems where a relatively small intervention can have a dramatic impact. It could be a steady drip that eventually bursts the dam, the proverbial straw that breaks the camel's back or some other tipping point. Better still, it is a relatively simple positive intervention that is reinforced so enthusiastically that it has a game-changing impact.

People are a dynamic asset

Would you like a pound for every time you've read or heard the CEO say, "Our people are our greatest asset"? How confident would these same CEOs be if someone had the temerity to say, "Prove it"? Of course, there's no reason why employees cannot be an organisation's greatest asset, and in many companies they are. But the truth is employees are a dynamic asset. The value of their contribution can go down as well as up, and that depends on, among other things:

- How they are managed
- The line-of-sight between their job, their team goals and organisational objectives
- How they perceive and relate to the customer
- How they perceive reward and whether they can influence it
- How they are learning and developing
- How they are involved in decisions that might affect them

We'll look at these and other issues as we continue our examination of the engagement system.

4. IT'S HOW THINGS ARE AROUND HERE

Wherever your organisation operates, employee engagement has to work within and be reflective of culture. To understand what impact that might have, we need to take a closer look at what we mean by culture and the level at which we are experiencing it.

Culture comes from the Latin word meaning cultivation. Originally an agricultural term, it was transformed at some point in its history to meaning being cultivated in the sense of refinement—in manners, in thought, in taste. More recently, we also use the social anthropological definition, which refers to the way that people feel, act and think in collective groups. This can be national, ethnic, religious, organisational or gender-specific. It is this latest definition with which we will concern ourselves.

Human culture

In one sense, human culture is universal. Much has remained with us since the time of the hunter-gatherers: a wish to belong to groups (and to decide who doesn't belong), fighting with other groups for territory or sustenance, and competition for partners. Those groups had their hierarchy, their morals and their gender roles.

At this level, most societal programming happens in childhood, when children are most receptive to learning and adaptive to their circumstances. They learn from parents, siblings, friends and extended family. Much of that learning will be conditioned by their environment and how people adapt to it. Is there food and shelter; are they in a threatening or unsafe environment; are they rich in resources? Our human culture developed over time, but its purpose was to help society survive through organisation and control, reducing uncertainty and focusing on common goals.

National culture

"Culture is more often a source of conflict than of synergy. Cultural differences are a nuisance at best and often a disaster."—Hofstede, Ph.D., Emeritus Professor, Maastricht University

The world is constantly changing around geopolitical, ethnic or religious associations. There are more than 200 nation states, and they all have their differentiators, some of which are unique. A large country like China has regions that are culturally different from each other while existing under a larger Chinese culture with the same constituent elements. African nations may be culturally similar but divided politically. In national cultures, the differences exist at an almost subconscious level in that people's beliefs, mores and understanding of what is acceptable were learned in childhood. This is why cultural differences between countries still persist despite the potentially unifying attributes of cheap air travel and satellite television. Failing to understand these cultural differences could lead to some very embarrassing moments when trying to do business—or enjoy a vacation.

Geert Hofstede has researched national differences in culture extensively and found four key dimensions in which differences exist. These were later augmented to six after research by Michael Bond (2002) and Michael Minkov (2010).

The cultural dimensions are:

- Power distance: the extent to which people in organisations accept that power is distributed unequally

- Uncertainty avoidance: society's tolerance for uncertainty and ambiguity
- Individualism: the degree to which people are integrated into groups (collectivism) or working alone
- Masculinity (versus femininity): the distribution of emotional roles in society
- Long-term orientation: long-term societies foster pragmatic virtues focused on long-term reward, while short-term societies foster values of the past and present like fulfilling obligations and maintaining dignity
- Indulgence versus restraint: relatively free gratification of human drives versus more self-control

Differing Dimensions

Power distance scores are high for Latin, Asian and African countries, and lower for Anglo and Germanic countries.

Uncertainty avoidance scores are higher in Latin countries, in Japan, and in German-speaking countries and lower in Anglo, Nordic, and far eastern countries like China and Singapore.

Individualism prevails in developed and Western countries, while collectivism prevails in less developed and Eastern countries; Japan takes a middle position on this dimension.

Masculinity is high in Japan and in some European countries like Germany, Austria and Switzerland. It is moderately high in Anglo countries, low in Nordic countries and in the Netherlands, and moderately low in some Latin and Asian countries like France, Spain and Thailand.

Long-term orientation scores are highest in East Asia; moderate in Eastern and Western Europe; and low in the Anglo world, the Muslim world, Latin America and Africa.

Indulgence scores are highest in Latin America, parts of Africa, the Anglo world and Nordic Europe; restraint is mostly found in East Asia, Eastern Europe and the Muslim world.

The impact of national culture will be almost invisible if you operate in one country. It is a given; it is programmed in. Operating in a number of countries requires an appreciation of the differences and making allowances for them. While national culture will dominate, it does not mean that different organisations in the same country have similar cultures.

Organisational culture

Most readers of this book work in organisations. We spend a considerable amount of time there, and we have learned what to do to fit in—what is acceptable and what is encouraged or frowned upon. We also almost subconsciously know how to act in a given situation. Organisations in the same country will have common national traits but will differ in their practices—rites, rituals, stories, vocabulary. This may be driven by organisational history, strong leadership, organisational values, market dynamics, systems and processes, the reward structure, and so on.

Where national cultures are a study within anthropology, organisational culture fits within sociology. Companies operating on a worldwide basis will recognise that national culture trumps organisational culture; therefore, a homogenous culture across the globe is almost impossible. What is possible is a shared understanding of operational goals, values and core ideology, if properly managed.

Within organisations there are three possible levels of culture; the deepest is rooted in the environment, human nature and relationships, and the current reality, and is driven mainly by national culture. The next level is supported by beliefs, values and attitudes, which drive the key behaviours important to organisational success. From here, companies develop and uphold the rites, rituals, heroes, ceremonies, stories and jokes that enrich organisational life. This also helps to explain why in one organisation there may be perceived differences in culture between, for example, sales and finance, or marketing and production. At the fundamental level, they are the same; at the second level, departmental or occupational imperatives start to kick in; at the third, more superficial level, they may indeed be different.

There is often confusion between the terms culture and climate in this context. They are related but not the same.

Climate refers to the beliefs and attitudes employees have about their organisation. Climate studies in the 1970s posited that employees experience climate, which influences their behaviour. Studies at this time found that, within any organisation, there was little agreement among employees about what it was like to work there, and so a more sophisticated way of looking at organisational life was sought (Brown, 1995).

To differentiate, culture is a relatively deep-rooted enduring state that can only be developed or changed over a lengthy period of time; climate operates at a more superficial (but no less real) level but can be changed fairly quickly with the right interventions. (Notice the plural. You can't do just one thing to effect change in a dynamically complex adaptive system.) Many 'culture change' initiatives over the last couple of decades were discredited because the culture actually didn't need changing. What was required very often was simply refocusing behaviours in support of core values.

Michael Michalko, who has written a number of books on creative thinking, tells a tale of "Five Monkeys" that is particularly apt in this context. (http://creativethinking.net/articles/index.php?s=The+Five+monkeys)

Start with a cage containing five monkeys. Inside the cage, hang a banana on a string and place a set of stairs under it. Before long, a monkey will go to the stairs and start to climb towards the banana. As soon as he touches the stairs, spray all the monkeys with ice cold water. After a while, another monkey makes an attempt with the same result—all the monkeys are sprayed with ice cold water. Pretty soon, when another monkey tries to climb the stairs, the other monkeys will try to prevent it.

Now, turn off the cold water. Remove one monkey from the cage and replace it with a new one. The new monkey sees the banana and will want to climb the stairs. To his surprise, all of the other monkeys attack him. After another attempt and attack, he knows that if he tries to climb the stairs he will be assaulted.

Next, remove another of the original monkeys and replace it with a new one. The newcomer goes to the stairs and is attacked. The previous newcomer takes part in the punishment with enthusiasm.

Again, replace a third monkey with a new one. The new one goes to the stairs and is attacked. Two of the four monkeys that beat him have no idea why they were not permitted to climb the stairs, or why they are participating in the beating of the newest monkey.

After new monkeys take the places of the fourth and fifth monkeys, all of the monkeys that were sprayed with cold water have been replaced. Nevertheless, no monkey ever again approaches the stairs. Why not? Because, as far as those monkeys know, that's the way it's always been done around here.

That, my friends is organisational culture!

Classifications

The growing interest in organisational culture bred a plethora of activity around trying to identify culture types so that any organisation could effectively be pigeonholed into one of (usually) four classifications. Those leading the charge included Harrison (1972), Handy (1978, 1985) building on Harrison's work, Deal and Kennedy (1982), Quinn and McGrath (1985), and Scholz (1987).

To give you a flavour, the Harrison/Handy characterisations are the *power culture*, the *role culture*, the *task culture* and the *person culture*. These deal with the different ways in which organisations are structured, how work is organized, lines of authority, responsibility, key focus, and flexibility.

Deal and Kennedy characterize cultures by focusing on the marketplace in which organisations operate and the degree of risk they take in transacting their business, as well as the speed at which they receive feedback on their decisions and strategies. Their classifications are the *tough-guy macho culture*, the *work hard/play hard culture*, the *bet-your-company culture* and the *process culture*.

Slotting your company into any one of these eight classifications may be difficult, and Deal and Kennedy at least would concede that. Admittedly, more knowledge of these classifications would be required before you could make a decision, and even then you would probably think, "I can see that aspect in our make-up, but we also fit into this other model." For our purposes, it is useful to be aware that that body of work is out there, and it is worth exploring. But for the immediate engagement imperative, it will be quicker and probably more productive to ask yourself a few questions about your organisation. Here are 10 for a starter:

1. How would you describe your culture to a potential recruit?
2. If you had to come up with a metaphor to describe your organisation, what would it be?
3. What events or achievements does the organisation celebrate?
4. What sort of rites and rituals does it indulge in?
5. What stories or jokes form part of the fabric of the organisation?
6. What are the espoused values? Are people "living" them?
7. Are there any corporate heroes who are celebrated?
8. To what extent do you encourage risk-taking?
9. What behaviours are rewarded?
10. Are you able to identify recognizable subcultures? Where are they? Can they be supported within the dominant culture?

Occupational culture

Occupational cultures are not necessarily a level down from organisational culture. Certainly—in the case of lawyers, doctors, actuaries, architects, and teachers—heroes, symbols, and rituals exist. Ethical standards are imposed, and qualification requires dedication to the vocation as well as academic standards. In that sense, they fall between national and organisational cultures in that what is demanded of them, or the way they act in a given situation, may not at first sight be supportive of the organisation, but it will be true to their calling. For that reason, you will sometimes witness conflict between hospital management and medical staff, the human resources or marketing staff with the partners in an accountancy firm, the civilian employees and the uniformed staff in the police force, communication practitioners and actuaries. For example there could be tension between what a doctor believes is the right course and timing of treatment for her patient; and the resources and budgetary constraints placed on her by administrators.

Generational considerations

In recent years, organisations have become accustomed to dealing with issues of diversity in the workplace. This started in the 1970s with equal pay for women. More recently, multiculturalism has become prominent. Deciding how to accommodate and deal with language barriers and different ethnic groups and religious beliefs in the workplace is now commonplace. One area that has more recently come on to the corporate radar is generational differences. Some organisations likely have employees from three different generations. Below are three commonly used characterisations.

Boomers, born between 1946 and 1964, tend to have a strong work ethic and understand the concept of loyalty to a company, unless of course they have been down-sized late in their career. They offer respect based on track record, and they're keen to show that their efforts have made a difference. They will embrace new technologies, but as an addition to their way of doing things, not necessarily as a replacement for them. New ideas may be perfectly acceptable, but they will still respect history and tradition. Many Boomers have retired or are thinking about retirement in the next few years. This will leave a skills gap as this generation is much larger than the one following it.

People categorized as Generation X, as they have been dubbed, were born between 1965 and 1979. They question authority and will give careful consideration, and maybe even do some basic research, before making decisions. They will not necessarily buy in to your new strategy or programme no matter how well it is promoted. They will look behind the message and the intent, and take advice from peers and associates while looking for evidence of the plan's credibility. When they grew up, there was more openness in the media, and investigative journalism was exploding a few myths and sacred cows. They are therefore more cynical by nature. They don't expect integrity, but they value it highly.

The Millennials, born between 1980 and 2000, sometimes referred to as Generation Y, are more optimistic and ambitious than their Generation X counterparts. Their focus is on their career, and any period of employment, however engaging, is a job. They will be focused and give of their best, but they won't tolerate any nonsense in the workplace; they will move on readily. Work-life balance is an issue for them because the time and space for leisure is very important. Millennials are heavily influenced by their peers. They want to be part of a large social group with similar interests, but they also look for a degree of individualism, for ways to emphasize their personality. They live in a world of immediacy—text, Twitter, Facebook—they make arrangements on the run. Jokingly, they don't know what they want, but they want it now. For this generation, diversity is not an issue; they expect it.

It takes more than a single solution to engage this diversity of generations in the workplace. Policies and procedures have to be more flexible, and the ways in which we communicate have to be adapted. There are plenty of media options, perhaps so many that it becomes confusing. There is certainly merit in not overcomplicating communication tactics. It is imperative to understand where the generations are cognitively, attitudinally and behaviourally through dialogue so that we can bring them where we need them to be.

External factors

Organisations make decisions based on a number of factors, the majority of which are external forces:

- Customer demand
- Competitive activity
- The economy

- The political environment
- Technological advances

All of these factors conspire to create the playing field and, to some extent, the rules for doing business. It is against this background that an organisation constructs its strategy, which will influence everything inside the organisation. This leads us to consider how people experience the organisational system and its subsystems.

5. DANCING WITH AN ELEPHANT

The organisational system recognises and drives the relationship between the organisation and the people who comprise it. While the organisation *is* people, over time it will have developed a personality that allows it to change but to endure through product life-cycles and changes in leadership and personnel. This determines the employment experience from first contact to exit. The way that people experience the organisation and its subsystems determines the extent to which they are engaged at any given time.

Typically, at least in Western society, we have adopted a reductionist approach, breaking issues down into their components and dealing with each in isolation. For us this is business-as-usual, stable, predictable, able to be planned (even change). This puts stress on the separate working parts (as do interventions) and can lead to fragmentation and an "either/or" mentality because what is valued is certainty and predictability. It's easy to see how this happens. Organisations are divided into functions, which are then subdivided into departments. Each department and function has a budget and projects to complete, and so a lot of work in organisations can be done in comparative isolation.

A systemic approach looks at the bigger picture and critically dependent issues. While this puts more emphasis on relationships and integration, it can also foster teamwork and experimentation. This approach can generate a "both/and" rather than an "either/or" mentality. It should produce a whole that is greater than the sum of its parts.

The experiential system has been represented here (Fig 5.1) to help us understand what it is we are trying to wrestle with in creating engagement.

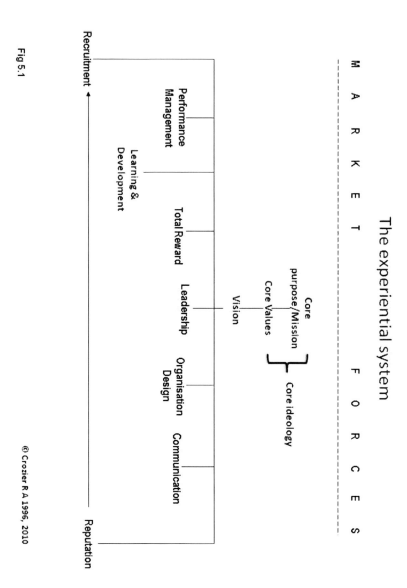

The experiential system

MARKET FORCES

Recruitment

Performance Management

Learning & Development

Total Reward

Leadership

Organisation Design

Communication

Vision

Core Values

Core purpose/Mission

Core ideology

Reputation

Fig 5.1

© Crozier R A 1996, 2010

As already discussed, on a daily or weekly basis, everything that happens inside the organisation is being influenced by something happening outside of it. But some things should not change.

Mission

Vision, mission and values often roll off the tongue as if they were indistinct. Vision and mission are often confused and almost interchangeable, and values are seen as things that exist on posters. Vision is for the heart, mission for the head, and values for the hands is a frequently quoted simplification. Let's look at this in more detail and in the logical order.

Mission or core purpose is the organisation's reason for being. This should not be confused with making money or specific business strategies that are deployed from time to time. In fact, focusing on money will probably result in failure of the strategic intent. The core purpose is more fundamental, and it endures over time. Having a deep-rooted purpose does not guarantee continual success, but it does help focus on what is important when times are tough.

Walt Elias Disney's greatest creation was not Snow White, Mickey Mouse, Disneyland, or the EPCOT Center; it was the core purpose upon which the Walt Disney Company was founded: to make people happy. Despite serious problems, including a cash-flow crisis in 1939 that occasioned a public offering and a takeover bid in the 1980s, the company managed to survive because it couldn't be carved up to realise value. It was more than a brand; it was woven into the fabric of U.S. society. Disney played an important role in the lives of children, and in addition to being seen as making people happy, it celebrated U.S. values. The Walt Disney Company is a very different entity today than it was when it was formed in 1923, but its core purpose endures.

The core purpose or mission of an organisation should not be driven by the current business strategy. Strategies will change over time to suit the prevailing market conditions. The mission should be able to last for 100 years or more. In constructing such a statement, the current products, services or strategies will be limiting. If Walt Disney had decided he was in the animation business, there wouldn't be a Walt Disney Company today. Neither would Sony still exist if it had stayed in the rice cooker business rather than "applying technology for the benefit of the public."

Engagement factors:

- Employees know and understand the core purpose of the organisation
- Employees know what they can do to support that core purpose
- Employees are committed to that purpose

Values

An organisation's core values are an essential set of firmly held beliefs that act as guiding principles for those inside the organisation. Core values are not driven by market forces, business strategies or management fads, and as such they are timeless. Different organisations may use similar words in their values statements, but what is important is that they understand what they philosophically believe to be the underpinning purpose for any value—what makes it unique for them—and what behaviours they expect to see from their people in support of that value. There is no *right* set of values; they must be individually constructed and sincerely held. What is vitally important is that an organisation has a set of values by which it lives, and that those values influence the policies, processes and behaviours adopted by the organisation in going about its business.

In a 1995 survey (Digital/MORI), 82 percent of the 497 senior executives polled said they believed that properly implemented, values contribute to profitability. Two-thirds of managers said they have had formal communication on values either through personal discussion or published material, and significantly, only 5 percent said that there has been no formal communication, but if you worked there you couldn't help knowing them. The significance of the latter figure is that the most effective means of communicating action-conditioning values is through observable behaviour.

In their book, *Built to Last*, Collins and Porras (1994) provide a great example of a company working its way through a values conversation with an executive group.

Debating whether to put "quality" on its list of core values, the CEO asked:

> "Suppose in ten years quality doesn't make a hoot of a difference in our markets. Suppose the only thing that matters is sheer speed and horsepower, but not quality. Would we still want to put quality on our list of core values?" The members of the management team looked around at each other and finally said, "To be honest, no." Quality stayed off the list as a core value. Quality stayed in the current strategy of the company—and quality improvement programmes remained in place as a mechanism for stimulating progress—but it did not make the list of core values. Remember, strategies change as market conditions change, but core values remain intact in a visionary company. This same group of executives then wrestled with whether it should put "leading-edge innovation" on its list of core values. The CEO asked the same question: "Would we keep it on the list as a core value, no matter how the world around us changes?" This time, the management team gave a resounding, "Yes! We always want to do leading-edge innovation. That's who we are. It's really important to us, and always will be. No matter what. And if our current markets don't value it, we will find markets that value it." Leading-edge innovation went on the list of core values, and will stay there forever. A company should not change its core values in response to market changes; rather, it should change markets—if necessary—in order to remain true to its core values. (p. 223)

Imagine then the confusion that can be caused when an organisation decides to re-brand: logo, font, strap line, and they throw core values into the mix. To make matters worse, it is all handled by the marketing department. The first part of the sentence above—brand, logo, and its articulation is perfectly legitimate. These things can be affected by the market and are the domain of the marketing department. If the issue is just about brand values, that is also fair game. But influencing or changing core values is tantamount to corporate delinquency. Core values may influence brand values, but brand values, susceptible to market forces and zeitgeist as they are, should not influence or change core values. If they do so, the espoused values will be seen internally as a cynical marketing ploy with no application for the people in the business, thereby obviating the function for which they should have been established.

If an organisation is establishing a statement of values for the first time, it can go about it in one of two ways: have a small number of key personnel with a lot of experience in the organisation representing different levels and departments come together to hammer out what is really important, or involve the whole organisation in focused dialogue on the issue over a period of time with a determined end point. Each has its advantages. The first can mean a speedy resolution, but there is then a big job to be done in gaining buy-in from the rest of the population, which takes time and budget. The second is slower but because all feel they have been involved, there is in-built buy-in. This also takes time and budget but in different proportions.

Collins and Porras (1994) also posit that taken together, core purpose and core values form the core ideology for the organisation. That, they argue, is the main driver in visionary companies. Organisations with a core ideology have endured over many years despite the slings and arrows of fluctuating fortune. Companies they cite include Disney, IBM, Sony, Hewlett Packard, 3M, Johnson & Johnson and Nordstrom. The model has two imperatives: preserve—core purpose and core values—and change—cultural and operating practices, specific goals, and strategies. These are not competing imperatives but a good example of "both/and" rather than "either/or."

Engagement factors:

- Understanding what the values mean
- Recognising that values influence policies
- Seeing that values influence behaviours
- Recognising that the manager "lives" the values
- "Living" the values (or not) will influence reward

Vision

This simple word is often misunderstood in an organisational context, and is frequently used as a substitute for mission. This may be because the vision has two components: the core ideology, which doesn't change, and the envisioned future, which can change. Unlike the core ideology, which could be around forever, the vision will consist of some audacious goals over a 10 to 25 year period. The vision has to be clearly articulated in vivid detail so that people can really imagine what it will be like working in that environment to achieve these goals. This is a significant challenge for leadership as they seek to take their people with them on this journey.

Engagement factors:

- Clear articulation of the vision
- Understanding the vision
- Having a grasp of what the vision will be like in practice
- Feeling committed to embark on the journey

Leadership

There are thousands of books about leadership and the vital role it plays in organisational success. A lot has been written about leaders as visionaries who, by sheer drive, entrepreneurship or charisma, carry the business to unprecedented success. That role is obviously vital, but leaders retire and the organisation has to endure. For the purposes of our discussion, leader means any individual in the company who is responsible, in a practical sense, for other people.

People like a point of contact for information, support, help, guidance and, even albeit subconsciously, as a role model. The CEO may fulfil that role for many, but realistically that function is performed by one's immediate superior. He or she is the most trusted, respected and reliable source for all things corporate. These individuals are the key to the corporate climate and dominant logic, and so must be fully on side with the core purpose, values and vision—not just cognitively but attitudinally and behaviourally.

Nowadays, leaders, managers and supervisors do not command respect or following merely by the accomplishment of title or promotion. To secure and galvanize employee commitment, they must win the hearts and minds of employees. Force or coercion is counterproductive. When the valued assets of companies are the knowledge and competencies of their employees, these assets demand leadership rather than management. Employees want a leader to follow and a cause to get behind. Management is for process; leadership is for people. So what does this mean?

- Leadership behaviours have to be cultivated within the organisation to support the corporate direction
- Leaders need to paint a vivid picture of the future that engages people, highlighting and celebrating achievements along the way
- The desired behaviours have to be modelled from the top down
- There has to be a connection between the purpose and vision and the personal interests of employees
- All supervisors and managers must embrace their role as leaders to earn support and commitment from staff
- All leaders must be given the means to achieve the above

Engagement factors:

- Trust in leadership
- Confidence in leaders' decisions
- Leaders stating the reasons behind their decisions
- Leaders encouraging employee involvement
- Leaders "living" the values
- Leaders providing constructive feedback

Organisation design

Successful organisations recognise that how they are structured has a material influence on their ongoing success, and they manage this accordingly. In contrast, one of the material influencing factors on less successful organisations is that their structures do not support their goals and objectives. At the core of organisation design is strategy, and while strategy and therefore organisation design can change, we have to be mindful that the core purpose will not and cannot be compromised.

Up to this point, it is perfectly possible to look at the organisation in the abstract, but it is now necessary to look at where people fit into the picture, because whether an organisation is a bank, a computer manufacturer or indeed, a church, it will require the intervention of people.

External factors

Life would be simple for organisations if there were no external factors; however, we do not live in a vacuum. The regulatory regime at the core of society spreads its influence into organisations. Obviously the law of the land is a major consideration, but then there could be professional standards (e. g. Accountancy) or other industry regulation

e. g. (Banking); health and safety considerations e. g. (Oil & Gas) to be observed. Inevitably, this creates the need for a degree of consistency, but it does not need to be prescriptive. It is how individual organisations address this that differentiates them. The defining factor in this is culture.

Management and span of control

As organisations grow in size; there is a need to ensure focus. There is also a need for specialist skills, and it is at this point that ensuring alignment with the organisation's purpose and congruence in its subsystems is vital. A key part of doing this lies in how the organisation is structured. Where does authority lie? There are a number of models that can be drawn upon to determine appropriate organisation structure, but the following represent key and consistent themes:

1. Functional: where activity and people are focused around business functions
2. Product: where activity is focused around a single product, which can be a service as well as a specific item
3. Geographic: where all activities in a geographic region report to a central unit
4. Matrix: a complex system that is common when there are multiple reporting responsibilities; this is typical in a project-based environment
5. Process-centred: where the business is dependent entirely on a progressive, end-to-end process
6. Dual process: where there is an operational distinction between customer interaction and product development and production (sometimes called front-end/back-end organisations)
7. Hybrid: where organisations call upon different structures according to variables in their business model

A core component to all of this, however, is the need for clarity across the organisation, which involves ensuring clear and concise lines of communication. It is also important to factor in individual aspiration and expectation. In developing the optimum organisation structure, it is important to take into account that for most employees the opportunity for professional development is paramount.

While there is a natural focus on structure of the organisation in this context, we must not forget that the systems and processes put in place, often for governance purposes, also have an impact. Inappropriate decision-making levels or sign-off authority for example are areas where intentions of good governance can become major areas of obstruction and frustration in trying to enact business.

Engagement factors:

- The business is structured in a logical way to satisfy its markets
- It is clear where individuals and departments fit into the big picture
- Work processes are efficient and minimize frustration and stress
- Business processes support the culture and purpose of the organisation

Performance management

Performance management is a strategic and integrated approach to delivering sustained organisational success by improving the performance of the people who work in the organisation and by developing the capabilities of teams and individual contributors (Armstrong & Bacon, 1998). Used effectively, performance management can integrate and align organisational, team and individual objectives. It can link functions in different parts of the business with strategic imperatives. Personal development and links to rewards can be accommodated within the system to help deal with people's individual aspirations.

Properly executed, performance management encourages individuals to manage their performance. It requires a management style that is open and honest, encouraging two-way communication between employee and supervisor. Performance is assessed against jointly agreed-upon goals on a regular basis so that there are no surprises at the end of the year. The performance management system should apply to all in the organisation, and it should be fair and transparent. It should not be seen primarily as a way of linking performance to rewards, but the link should exist.

Engagement factors:

- Employees know what is expected of them
- They have an opportunity to influence their objectives
- They can determine how their work gets done
- There is a clear line of sight between individual, team and organisational goals
- There are clear links between performance and reward
- Performance reviews help people to improve and develop

Total rewards

The way employees are rewarded in an organisation is a mixture of several components. There will be a market rate for the job, and account will be taken of the skills and competencies of the individual as well as the contributions they make. This will be done in the context of a reward philosophy, which may be driven by the market. Some organisations state that base pay will be market median, but total compensation will be in the upper quartile. Others may opt for upper quartile pay and upper decile total compensation.

Total compensation is the sum of extrinsic and intrinsic rewards. Extrinsic rewards usually have an identifiable cash sum attached to them: base pay plus incentives or bonuses, pension contributions, shares, insurances and holidays. Intrinsic rewards include development, recognition, the work itself, career opportunity, relationships, and the work environment.

There is a growing trend for organisations to promote the concept of total rewards so that employees know and understand the total value of their employment. Some have lost staff to competitors because the entirety of the reward package was not properly understood. Reward is an emotive issue, but Hertzberg's findings (1962) still hold true: it only becomes an issue when it is perceived as being below expectations. Consequently, some organisations invest significant sums in ensuring that their people know and understand the value of the pay and benefits with which they are provided. But some companies still get this very wrong.

A few years ago, an employee benefits consultancy, wishing to be seen as endorsing the services it sold to clients, heralded its own version of flexible benefits to employees. In effect, what it offered was one additional benefit and one benefit enhancement—both on a salary-sacrifice basis. The organisation concurrently changed its company car scheme to restrict eligibility. All of this was communicated in print. When the glossy "kit" arrived on people's desks, it was met with derision and a great deal of cynicism. It was not viewed as flexible, and the company's motives were questioned.

Another company, which stated that it valued its employees and had a philosophy of rewarding performance, announced an across-the-board annual pay increase by sending out a circular. These examples are not simply incongruent communication manifesting itself in a gap between rhetoric and reality; they represent a fundamental failure on the part of management to understand the symbiosis between all of the elements of the employment experience. Failure of that kind has much greater ramifications than immediate disillusionment. It feeds distrust, cynicism and de-motivation, and consigns the next corporate initiative, however worthy, to the realm of canteen humour.

A more powerful and positive piece of symbolic communication on rewards occurred a few years ago when Oki, the Japanese electronics company, set up a new facility in Cumbernauld, Scotland to manufacture computer peripherals, mainly printers and ink cartridges. The plant did very well in a relatively short period of time, and when he thought it would be the right time financially, the Scottish human resources director suggested to the Japanese managing director that they should seriously consider giving all staff in the plant a bonus for their achievements. They discussed this and agreed on bonus amounts. The managing director then asked how they should make these payments. The HR director thought that they should be paid with salary directly into employees' bank accounts.

"But how will they know that we appreciate what they have achieved?" asked the managing director. He decided to hand over a cheque to each employee personally to thank them and let them know their efforts were valued.

How's that for impact?

Work-life balance and the psychological contract

There is another dimension to the employment experience that is often overlooked, particularly from the outside. As companies have de-layered and "right-sized," hierarchy is not the only thing that has disappeared. There has also been a loosening of the bond between employer and employee. This has had two opposite effects. On one hand, people may become totally disaffected and de-motivated, adopting an "I'm not paid to do that" philosophy. On the other hand, some people, after looking around at the corporate carnage, decide to put their noses to the grindstone and work longer, if not harder, to give the necessary impression of commitment.

A number of companies have been happy to endorse this latter behaviour since they can see the benefits of additional work at no additional cost. Such behaviours are seen as rewarding and very quickly become accepted as the norm. Normal mortals working the contractual hours are not viewed as being committed, and this psychological contract is reinforced. "Enough" is not determined by the length of the working day but by the limits of human endurance (Kanter, 1989).

More enlightened companies are prepared to accept that, however talented, people work most effectively for limited periods of time with decent breaks. They promote a more civilized way of working and reward achievement rather than "presenteeism," recognizing that complete human beings, with a work, social and family life, are more valuable than the corporate automatons they could so easily have bred.

The term "psychological contract" was originally coined in the 1960s by Argyris and Levinson to describe the subjective nature of the employer-employee relationship. It is used in contemporary times to refer specifically to the employee's belief in and perception of a contractual promise whether or not it is formally laid out (Hiltrop, 1995). As such, these contracts fulfil two main purposes: They define the employment relationship, and they manage mutual expectations. Employers can define the inputs and outputs expected from employees, and they in turn, expect rewards for their efforts. It is impossible to spell all of this out at the time of striking the employment contract as so much of the actual relationship is cultural.

Security for individuals nowadays does not come from being employed but from being employable (Kanter, 1989). Longevity for companies will come from their own ability to recruit, reward (in every sense) and retain the highly desirable, talented employees who want to work with them. While work-life balance is often cited as an attractor to a company, it rarely shows up in research as a reason for leaving.

Engagement factors:

- The reward policy is clear and understandable
- Base pay is at least on market
- Incentive arrangements can boost total pay
- People feel they can influence their rewards
- People know and understand the value of their total package
- People believe the reward system is fair

Learning and development

Everyday life in an organisation influences people to develop existing skills and learn new ones, including the work-related tasks or projects employees are involved in and what they pick up from colleagues in terms of attitude and behaviour. For some careers, there is a prescribed course of learning, study and examination, which is formalised and controlled.

For the organisation to benefit in the long term from its collective learning, it has to capture new knowledge, experiences, techniques and understanding. This forms the organisational memory people can tap into for insights and solutions. It also enhances structural capital.

On an individual level, people are encouraged to take charge of their own learning and development so that they acquire the knowledge, skills, and competencies most relevant to them and their career path. This of course has to fit in with organisational requirements but is predicated on the principle of future employability. The process is supported in the performance management system where there is an opportunity to discuss aspirations and development opportunities. In many cases, this is augmented by a mentoring system. Lack of personal development opportunities is frequently cited by people who are considering leaving their present employment.

Engagement factors:

- Employees have the training and tools to do their jobs well
- Professional development needs are being identified
- Learning and development is encouraged and supported
- Interesting projects or new work experiences are identified for development purposes

Communication

The need for communication pervades all of the above and is implicit in the success of any corporate initiative. Unfortunately, even when the need for communication is recognised, it is more often than not at a tactical level. Communication is not simply a management tool to be plugged in to the back of an issue to give it energy. This misapprehension comes about from confusing *information* and *communication*. Information is the raw material; communication is the process applied to it to give it relevance and value. While information and communication are different, they are inextricably related. Communication is not a tool to aid business; business is largely about communication.

According to Mehrabian (1971), only seven percent of what is perceived from communication is verbal. Thirty-eight percent is derived from the paralinguistics (style, manner, tone, medium) and fifty-five percent from body language. It is impossible therefore for individuals in a company not to communicate. Holding back information, failing to enter dialogue or being less than proactive still sends a message—almost certainly not the right one.

There is now a plethora of evidence to support the assertion that effective communication can positively affect engagement in concert with the other sub-systems, but communicating in one dimension will only influence awareness and understanding. Gaining acceptance, motivation and commitment requires the interpersonal involvement of people at all levels as well as the alignment and congruence of the other sub-systems. Because communication has a disproportionate role among the subsystems, we will give it its own space in Chapter 6.

Engagement factors:

- Creating awareness and understanding
- Providing the context for issues
- Involvement and dialogue
- Acting on feedback
- Role-modelling the desired behaviours

Recruitment

Recruitment is at the sharp end of the human resources planning process. The "hard" numbers ensure that the desired number of the right sort of people are available when required. The "softer" piece is concerned with formulating the culture so that the employee values, beliefs and behaviours are aligned with those of the organisation, thereby contributing to organisational goals. This takes us neatly back to recruiting the right sort of people.

The recruitment process for many will be their first real encounter with the organisation. Because views formed at this time will stay with them for a while, it is incumbent on those responsible to portray the organisation in a good light. Stories abound about people applying for jobs and not even receiving an acknowledgement. What does that tell us? Valued assets? In many instances, the most junior people in human resources are assigned to recruitment; that is like putting the least experienced person on the reception desk. Not long after coming through the recruitment process themselves, they can be more occupied with process than hiring quality. This is also where, too often, we find the person responsible for the employer brand. At this level, they are selling the employment prospect, not building the employment experience (i.e., selling three-pointed stars, not building a Mercedes). The employment experience has to be built from the top.

Whatever clever advertising or promotion is done to attract candidates, however sophisticated and scientific the selection process, organisations must pay attention to the human side of the process and accord respect to individuals. A rejected candidate could still be an advocate for the organisation.

Engagement factors:

- Staff involved portray the culture and values throughout the recruitment process
- People are kept informed on a timely basis throughout the process
- Recruitment advertising in all media accurately reflects the (real) employer brand

Reputation

The best organisations promote, guard and protect their identity. They work very hard to manage the way they are perceived and assiduously nurture their reputation. In a crisis situation, the company with a good reputation will handle the situation proactively and professionally, considering all of its stakeholders or constituencies. At worst, it will have to make a small withdrawal on its goodwill. A company with a more defensive approach in the same situation will take a severe dent to its image from which it may never recover. But while identity can be in an organisation's control, image and reputation rely on third-party experience.

In his book *Reputation* (1996), Charles Fombrun puts employees at the top of his list of constituencies to be addressed in creating a good corporate reputation. He quotes the authors of *The Hundred Best Companies to Work for in America*, "Despite the diversity, almost every one of the 100 Best has something distinctive to offer its employees" (p. 112).

While the authors of the 100 Best recognised that each company is unique, there were consistent themes that they came across time and time again. Synthesizing their comments, employees favour companies that promote trust, empower their people and inspire pride.

Reputation is experienced internally as well as externally. The external perception will aid the recruitment process, but there is sometimes incongruence between the corporate or product brand and the employer brand. There has to be synergy and harmony for lasting success.

Enron looked like a good prospect for investment and employment between 1985 and 2000. Strong on image, mission and values. But it was hiding a dirty secret. Billions of dollars in debt from failed deals and projects were hidden by accounting loopholes and special purpose entities. When the balloon burst in October 2001, the stock price had fallen from $90.00 in mid 2000 to $1.00. Enron filed for bankruptcy under Chapter 11 of the US Bankruptcy code; at the time the biggest in US history.

Many executives at Enron were indicted for a variety of charges and ended up in prison. Employees and shareholders received limited returns in lawsuits, despite losing billions in pensions and stock prices. So not only did employees lose their jobs, they lost their pension savings.

People energize organisations and bring them to life. The way that people act, interact and react in the pursuit of a common purpose creates the climate and culture in an organisation to support its objectives. These same people deliver goods and services to the marketplace and help or wholly condition the organisation's reputation.

Engagement factors:

- The organisation is well known and respected in its sector
- It produces quality products and/or offers quality services
- It has strong performance
- The quality of its personnel is high
- It is socially responsible

Employer brand

"Employer branding is the process of creating an identity and managing the image of an organisation in its role as an employer." (Crozier R A, Total Employment Relationship Management, Fairleigh Dickinson University, 1998, p.70)

This requires a holistic or systemic approach which means that organisations have to take care of the total employment experience, not just part of it. Consideration has to be given to all of the ways in which the enterprise, in its various pursuits, interacts with its people—as described in this chapter. Ideally that starts before the recruitment process and does not necessarily end as the period of employment ends. In today's market it should be feasible for the parties to work together again at some point for mutual benefit—assuming of course that the employment experience was conducive to that.

While there may be few written definitions of employer branding, there are more interpretations in practice. Perhaps not surprisingly as this notion emerged, businesses promoted their particular view of what it meant. The recruitment sector saw it as an opportunity to re-energise advertising and promotion of their clients as valid destinations for talent. This is a perfectly legitimate thing to do but runs the risk of creating a gap between rhetoric and reality if the employment experience does not live up to the promise. This was effectively branding the employment *proposition*, not the employment experience.

Some in the employee benefits business sought to get involved in what they called *employment* branding; in effect it was packaging the employment "deal" which tended to concentrate on extrinsic and intrinsic reward.

In itself this is a vital function as people have to appreciate and value what they have in employment if companies are going to drive value from their investment.

One worrying manifestation is companies referring to the *employee* brand. Do they seriously want to create a population of automatons who so obviously belong to their organisation? Are they trying to confer some attributes of the corporate or product brand on their employees? If this is being done in the name of alignment between corporate, product and employer brands, then these organisations should describe it more appropriately.

Can you imagine telling today's employees they are being branded?

Thinking of the employer brand in a systemic way serves to highlight the importance of the engagement manifesto to create the brand from inside the organisation and then find the means to express it externally.

Engagement factors

- The employer brand is clearly aligned with business objectives
- The employment experience is consistent with the employment promise
- The brand is clearly articulated and understood
- The values are manifested in the brand
- The employer brand demonstrably helps attract talent

Why can't I just tick boxes?

Figure 5.1, which was used to help us examine the various subsystems looks admittedly like an organisation chart, but it's useful to help us understand the construct. Here is a more systemic view of the engagement construct (Fig 5.2).

Fig 5.2

The engagement system

The wheel represents the constituents of your organisation in functioning through your people. At the centre are your core purpose and core values as well as a vision of where they can take you. The values are pervasive, affecting every part of the entity. The organisation design determines how things get done, while communication oils the cogs and lubricates everything from the core to the policies, processes and behaviours that are in place in the outer ring to support goal achievement. This organisational system has volition, and it is self-sustaining. It's not rigid; it has fluidity. But what if you need to change something?

For example, suppose that many of your supervisors need better interpersonal communication skills to improve relationships and ultimately productivity on the shop floor. You may decide to organize workshops, a training course or some coaching to deal with this issue. Box ticked? Yes. Issue successfully resolved? No.

Imagine that what is holding your organisational system together and allowing it to self-sustain is an elastic band. It fits round the circumference of the model. We have decided that leadership and management have to take a different form, and so we have initiated an intervention to deal with it. We stretch the elastic band in that area to occupy a new position, and it is held there during the intervention with a pin. When the intervention is over and the pin is removed, the system reverts to the old shape. In the example of the supervisors, they possibly went back to their day jobs and tried something different only to be derided by their colleagues for having been on a brainwashing session or in a sheep-dip, and told, "that's not the way we work round here."

For an intervention to be successful, it has to be supported elsewhere in the system. There must be communication about the aims and objectives of the process, the desired outcomes and how everyone will benefit. Leaders must focus on the new behaviours in the performance management system and how they will be assessed, rewarding the people who successfully demonstrate the desired behaviours. Doing these things will ensure that the change is embedded and sustainable.

You may decide that going forward you need to recruit a different type of person into this role. Historically you have promoted good technicians, but now you recognise that you need a different skill set. You don't have to work your way around the model; you can cut straight through to influence the recruitment process as long as you communicate effectively, ensure that you are in line with the values and that your actions will support the core purpose.

We were invited by Clydesdale Bank, which has approximately 5,000 employees and is part of National Australia Group, to help them introduce a new bonus plan in keeping with the rest of the group, thereby reinforcing its pay for performance philosophy and rewarding those "who go the extra mile." Rather than charge ahead and develop a communication strategy to do that, we suggested conducting some research. Focus groups with junior staff and supervisors showed that any new bonus arrangement would be considered insulting and patronising since they were acutely aware that salary levels had fallen well below those of their competitors. And no one could understand what an "extra mile "looked like in practice.

The bank knew that there were salary anomalies among more junior staff and had in fact been working on a solution, but this response caused them to pause and rethink the strategy. The bonus arrangements were put on hold, and the bank concentrated on pay policy. Once a new policy had been designed and agreed on, the new remuneration strategy, which was visibly aligned to the market, and the staff appraisal system were launched. The new bonus arrangements, which were linked to performance (team and individual with no mention of an extra mile), were then introduced, followed by the policy and programme on career development. Finally, the organisation realigned its staff banking benefits.

This integrated rollout took only one year and was very successful, as evidenced by annual employee opinion survey results. The critical step was involving people at the outset. That effectively reordered the process, forcing the bank to step back from the presenting issue and deal with the other critical dependencies in the system. This approach brought success where others may have found costly failure. In fact, the initial single intervention strategy could have resulted in strike action.

6. DON'T MENTION THE C-WORD

Communication is universally understood yet not uniformly understood.

Many senior executives are not particularly interested in communication philosophy, but they are interested in business. It is important then that we do not agonise over getting "communication" on the agenda but demonstrate its effectiveness in supporting business objectives.

Commûnicâ'tion *n* (an act of) communicating; that which is communicated; (a piece of) correspondence; a means of communicating, a connecting passage or channel; (*in pl)* means of giving and receiving information, such as speech, telecommunications, the press, and cinema; a means of transporting, *esp* troops and supplies. (Chambers, 10th Edition, 2006).

The dictionary definition seems woefully inadequate, indeed almost inappropriate when considered in the context of organisational communication and what we hope to achieve by it, especially with engagement. So let's have some clarity. Engagement as defined in Chapter 2 is not the logical outcome of a communication process. Communication has a vital role to play in the engagement system, and we will explore that here, but it has to work in concert with the other subsystems.

When people talk about communication and engagement, it would seem that what they refer to is more accurately described as communication and involvement with a view to gaining a degree of commitment around certain issues. Most effort is put into finding the best channels and media for engaging *with* employees. That is quite different from what we describe here as employee engagement. Problems arise when we use the word engagement to mean different things—and the issue lies in the fact that not many organisations appreciate that difference. The best communication process in the world can't overcome poor leadership, inadequate rewards, a lack of development opportunities, or a culture that rewards tenure rather than performance. In those circumstances, people won't be engaged, and the communication function is powerless to change that. Unless the person with titular responsibility for engagement sits between the CEO and senior human resources staff (or is one of these people), there will be no serious influence, and it is at this level that responsibility for engagement must reside.

Meanwhile, there is a serious job to be done in supporting the organisation's engagement philosophy because employee engagement won't materialise without communication.

Principles or charter

For guidance, it is important that the organisation has some principles around communication and involvement or even a published charter. This typically includes five main elements:

1. Objectives: What will better communication and involvement deliver for the business? What will we be able to hear or see that tells us it is working? How can it support employee engagement, and what impact will it have?
2. Guiding principles: What are the things we believe are important? What is the bedrock to which we will anchor our communication behaviours? How will we demonstrate our values?
3. Channels and media: What channels and media will we consider? Which do we believe are most important? How open are we to innovative approaches and new technology?
4. Responsibility: Who is responsible for strategy, processes and activities? Do we have adequate resources to support

them? What are this person's responsibilities in the wider organisation?

5. Effectiveness: How will we evaluate our communication and involvement activities so that we know they are working as intended or make alterations to refocus them?

Based on the foregoing, the strategy should take shape. It may simply be a number of bullet-pointed statements of intent, but it will obviously support and manifestly demonstrate the objectives and principles established in the charter.

It could include, for example:

- Creating links between people's work and the overall business goals
- The role of leaders and managers
- Building trust and relationships
- Measures for communication and involvement
- Methods for providing context
- Ways to develop communication skills

The following is an actual example of how one company, through facilitated discussion using the model above, formulated its charter and strategy to support the wider employee engagement objectives.

-ooOoo-

Our charter

Objectives

Through focused and effective communication and involvement strategies and activities, as well as other people management practices, we aim to create a positive experience of working with (the company).

In practice, this will mean that people feel a sense of belonging to a company in which they can take pride - a place where people are treated as individuals and where they are aware of and understand what is expected of them and how they can contribute to the overall business objectives.

By having our people aligned with and committed to our goals, we expect to see people who are truly engaged with us. The resultant benefits might include the following:

- Increased job satisfaction
- Reduced turnover
- Enhancements in product/service delivery
- A strong employer brand
- The ability to attract talent
- Satisfied clients
- Happy shareholders

Guiding Principles for communication and involvement

We will communicate openly, honestly, and in a timely manner on issues affecting the organisation and its communities as a whole or in part.

We are committed to dialogue, being responsive to feedback and to having consistent communication across a number of channels and media.

Our aim is to be inclusive, recognising that there will be different interest groups and cultural sensitivities within (the company) and beyond that have to be accommodated.

We will use plain English as a universal standard and tailor our messages with the stakeholder in mind.

We will assume positive intent in all communication regardless of source and respond appropriately in line with these principles and our values.

Channels and media

We will use channels and media appropriate to the content, objective and stakeholder groups.

We will make effective use of face-to-face communication wherever appropriate, and we will encourage and support team-based communication whether on a formal or informal basis.

Communication in print and by electronic means will also be a regular feature of the sharing of information and opinions.

Channels and media will be regularly reviewed to ensure their effectiveness, and new media may be introduced when necessary.

Responsibility

Overall responsibility for the communication strategy will rest with human resources in partnership with management.

While the drive for communication will often come from senior management, it is the responsibility of all managers and team leaders to engage with their people in displaying integrity and consistency in the key messages.

Everyone in (the company) has a responsibility to communicate openly and honestly on all issues, and management has a responsibility to ensure that people feel free to do so without fear of negative repercussion. People are expected to participate constructively in this process.

Communication with and through external media will be the responsibility of nominated executives only.

Effectiveness

From time to time we will check the effectiveness of our communication and involvement processes and make adjustments as necessary.

We will use informal (feedback/comments/questions) and formal (e.g., surveys/focus groups) methods to achieve this, and we should be able to identify the impact on the areas set out in objectives.

The final test will be that we are trusted by our stakeholders, and they in turn become advocates for (the company).

Top-line Strategy

In order to support our strategy of improved communication and involvement; we will implement and embed our charter by focusing on:

- Creating positive links through dialogue with people to ensure they understand our key business objectives and how they relate to their jobs
- Ensuring that managers recognise the importance of communication in achieving business results by demonstrating the appropriate leadership behaviours
- Demonstrating strong leadership and commitment by driving through the implementation of the strategy
- Building trust and strong relationships between management and employees through increased face-to-face involvement
- Establishing clear objectives and measures for managers on communication effectiveness and rewarding them on their performance in that regard
- Providing ongoing and timely communication to all stakeholders to ensure they have the information, knowledge and context to enable them to do their jobs
- Developing our managers' communication skills

-ooOoo-

Managing communication is a critical skill for managers. The following are key principles they must remember:

1. It is impossible not to communicate: Not saying or doing something in a given situation still sends a message
2. Effective communication is determined by the recipient: By their understanding and actions, employees decide whether communication is effective
3. The more complex the issue, the greater the need for communication to be informal, frequent and interpersonal
4. Observed behaviours are the most powerful and reinforcing elements in underpinning expectations and the resultant actions in a workforce
5. Employees tolerate management's logic but act on their own conclusions

It's easy to fall into the trap of talking about the workforce or employees as if they were an amorphous mass. They are not. They can be differentiated by age, sex, beliefs, attitudes, skills, perceptions, qualifications, length of service, culture, values—and so on. This makes it all the more important for involvement to start with the immediate manager, the person who knows the individuals and their interests and concerns. The company's job is to support that with the purpose, values, vision, infrastructure and senior management commitment that effectively walks the organisational talk.

Simplifying the construct

In most organisations, more than 80 percent of what employees currently perceive or believe does not come from official communication channels. Every organisation has a grapevine. We can't obviate it, but we can make it more effective and less damaging. Why does the grapevine exist? It is fast, informal, interpersonal and focuses on "me" issues. Replicating these aspects in organisational communication can ensure that the official version of events is given more credence.

Sitting in an organisation and trying to penetrate the morass that organisational communication can seem to be is a daunting task. It would do no harm to simplify it into some manageable components.

Explicit communication: information, messages and feedback through visual, interpersonal, audiovisual, or e-media channels.

Implicit communication: culture, climate, values, observable behaviours and interactions, involvement, and the structure of policies and processes.

When it comes to managing communication, the well-worn continuum still works: a**wareness** → **understanding** → **acceptance** → **commitment** → **action.**

We can use it to good effect, but we need to have another structure in place to ensure that we communicate effectively. For that purpose, communication comprises four key elements: Feedback, Involvement, Role-modelling and Messaging (FIRM™).

Feedback: Everything you see in the organisation today is feedback from yesterday. Take that into account as a starting point, and then consider climate, attitudes, behaviours, opinions, results, dominant logic, survey data, focus groups, and one-to-one interactions.

Involvement: Involvement refers to involving people in decisions that might affect them or in which they have an interest—such as inclusion, diversity, socialisation consulting and conferring.

Role-modelling: Leadership and line managers are role models when they manifest the desired observable behaviours, live the organisation's values, and exhibit congruence between rhetoric and reality (high say: high do).

To explain further, consistency in word (say) and deed (do) is critical in driving trust and commitment. Mixed signals are interpreted as deceit, and employees speculate on scenarios fuelled by the grapevine, which results in low trust and a downward spiral in morale.

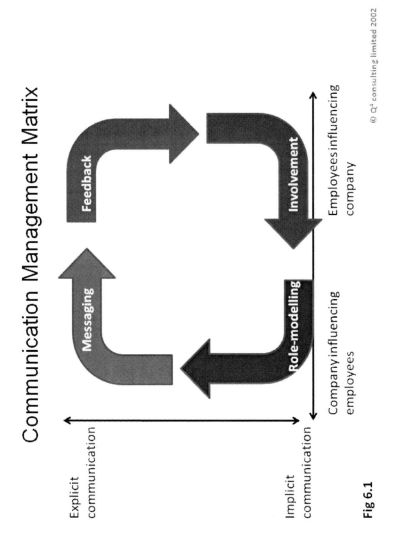

Communication Management Matrix

Feedback

Involvement

Messaging

Role-modelling

Explicit communication

Implicit communication

Employees influencing company

Company influencing employees

© Q⁴ consulting limited 2002

Fig 6.1

Messaging: Messaging encompasses key messages, information, style and mood, honesty, timeliness and targeting.

The model in Fig 6.1 can be used to start thinking about communication management. Messaging and feedback represent explicit communication, while role-modelling and involvement represent implicit communication. Messaging and role-modelling are the main ways in which the organisation influences employees; feedback and involvement are the ways in which employees can influence the organisation.

Thinking about a project in which communication plays a vital part, you can apply the FIRM™ model to the five-stage communication process (See Fig 6.2). For each stage of the process, decide which elements of the matrix apply and how you wish to apply them. The things you might want to consider are laid out in more detail in the next model, which you could turn into a template (Fig 6.3). The model applies to one stage or a combined stage (e.g., awareness/understanding) in the process so the exercise has to be repeated for the other stages.

Communication process overview

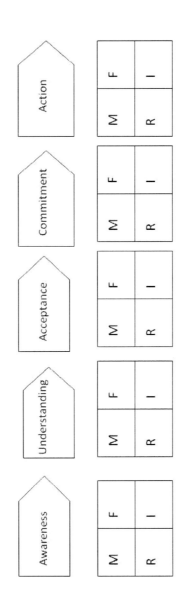

Awareness		Understanding		Acceptance		Commitment		Action	
M	F	M	F	M	F	M	F	M	F
R	I	R	I	R	I	R	I	R	I

Messaging; Feedback;

Role-modelling; Involvement;

F I R M™ Q² consulting limited 1999

FIG 6.2

Communication Planning Matrix

Issue/subject: **Stage:**   **Stakeholders:**   **Channels/media:**

What is the issue?   What stage are we at?   Who are we targeting?   How are we going to get to them?

Messaging	Feedback
What are the key messages at this stage?	What do we know about current perceptions and attitudes on this issue? What feedback are we looking for from this stage of the process and how will we get it?

Role-modelling	Involvement
What do we need to do to reinforce the message at this stage? What observable behaviours do we want to see exhibited?	How are we going to involve our stakeholders in this stage of the process?

Timing: When are we doing this? How long will it take?

Fig 6.3

FIRM™ Q⁴ consulting limited 1999

What is important is that all four aspects of the FIRM™ matrix are applied somewhere over the process, although not necessarily at every stage. Failure to do so runs the risk of not communicating effectively. It is also useful to think in advance about the sort of questions and issues that may be raised and to have a view of what success in dealing with them might look like (see Fig 6.4).

Linking communication and involvement strategy to organisational objectives requires a planning process. Typically, this would be carried out on an annual basis, but it has to be flexible enough to cope with unforeseen circumstances. The example in Figure 6.5 can be templated and repurposed for individual use.

Fig 6.4

Stage	What questions will people ask me?	Success measure
Awareness Making people aware of the issues and painting the big picture and process	What is the business direction? What role do I play in this? Will I be measured and rewarded differently? How does this help the company be more successful? What are the potential outcomes?	5. Understanding 4. 3. 2. 1. Confusion
Understanding Giving people a greater understanding of the issues and the context for the decision-making.	Why is this issue important? How will it be implemented? Why should I care about it? Do I support it?	5. Acceptance 4. 3. 2. 1. Resistance
Acceptance People start to see what it means for them and how they may be able to play a part.	How can I deal with this in my work? How does this affect my day to day activities? What stays the same and what changes? What do I need to do differently—or do I need to do different things? What is everyone else doing?	5. Commitment 4. 3. 2. 1. Decision not to implement
Commitment People start to focus on how they can make it happen and look for reassurance that everyone is playing their part.	Is all this consistent? Are resources invested and aligned? How committed are senior managers? Is everybody up for this? What will success look like? What are the visible outcomes? What are the rewards?	5. Personal change 4. 3. 2. 1. Aborted after implementation
Action People start to take ownership and are enthusiastic as it matches their goals, interests, and aspirations.	What else can I do to help? How can I help others? What's next?	5. It's how we do things around here.

Adapted from Ayelet Baron, IABC Handbook of Organizational Communication, (Jossey Bass) 2006

FIG 6.5 Communication planning template

Opportunity	Purpose	Participants	Frequency	Desired outcomes	Measures
Managing Director's presentation	To appraise people on business progress, achievements, Market conditions and future plans.	All employees	Annual	Awareness of issues and challenges facing the business. Understanding of continued necessity for change.	Quality of questions. Feedback at team meetings. Prompted awareness of issues.
Senior Management meeting	To clarify strategy and context. To plan implementation and agree outcomes.	Directors and Heads of Dept	Bi-monthly		
Department meetings					
Team meetings					
Newsletter					

Every business decision requires a communication decision. While decisions may not necessarily fit into the existing communication plan, they do require action. A simple template, like a communication decision matrix (Fig 6.6) can help you think through what needs to be done when a decision is made. If a decision is made at a meeting, those at the meeting should agree on the communication process and take responsibility for it. Once this process has been worked through a few times, it will become second nature. This ensures that communication is fast, focused, and relevant, getting out ahead of the grapevine. The terms are explained below:

Communication Decision Matrix

Every business decision requires a communication decision

Meeting: Date:

Issue/Decision	Stakeholders	Impact	Need to know	Medium	Timing	Who?	Feedback?

Fig 6.6

Meeting: board, executive management team, or any other authorized group convened to deal with specific issues.

Date: the date the meeting is held

Issue/decision: the issue or decision that requires wider dissemination

Stakeholders: those who will have an interest in this issue

Impact: What is the likely or desired impact of this decision or issue on each stakeholder group?

Need to know: What level of importance do we place on communicating with each stakeholder? For example:

1. **Enforced:** what we must communicate by law
2. **Essential:** what it is imperative to communicate
3. **Expected:** what people reasonably expect to know
4. **Expedient:** what we would like people to know

Decisions on these categories will affect timing and the media used.

Medium: How will we communicate with each stakeholder group, e.g., interpersonally*, via e-mail, on the intranet, in meeting minutes, etc.?

Timing: At or by what time will the communication have taken place?

Who: Which person or persons will be responsible for communicating about this issue?

Feedback: Is feedback on the issue required, and if so, how will we gather it?

Communication decisions made in these forums may then feed in to the communication plan.

*Interpersonal interactions include one-to-one conversations, buddying, group meetings, skip-level meetings, business breakfasts, and any forum, however informal, that encourages dialogue.

Dealing with major change

"There is nothing more difficult to carry out, nor more doubtful of success, nor more dangerous to handle, than to institute a new order of things."

—Machiavelli

Communicating in a steady state environment can be challenging enough, but what happens when there is a significant event that potentially could upset the apple cart?

Most corporate change initiatives fail in their strategic intent. The market average success rate for mergers and acquisitions in terms of driving value for shareholders is just 32.4 percent. And less traumatic change initiatives don't fair much better; over 60 percent of those fail to deliver on their promise. There is a common reason for this—insufficient attention to the human dimension of change. It is very easy to get wrapped up in the hard numbers and forget what is considered the "soft" stuff. But it's not soft; it's difficult. In fact, the hard numbers are the easy part. Not dealing with the people issues in change is what causes failure. There may be nothing wrong with the new acquisition or strategy per se, but if the people are not properly aligned behind the venture and committed to seeing it though, it's not going to drive value.

Five hundred and twenty of 531 CEOs polled by the Jensen Group in 1995 stated that they wished they had communicated better. Communication initiatives that are undertaken are often late; the grapevine has beaten them to it. They confuse information with communication and concentrate on messages not actions, forgetting (if they ever knew) that in this situation communication has to be frequent, informal and interpersonal. Senior leaders often think that they have communicated when the memo goes out. They need to get out in front of the process and be prepared to spend a lot of time explaining, answering questions and repeating the same messages until they are sick of stating them. Only then will people start to think it's for real. Failure to do so allows the grapevine or the unions to control the agenda, and that always exaggerates the negative. People become confused and de-motivated, and productivity suffers. Over time, value is destroyed.

In times of change, speed is of the essence. In a major change program, the first 100 days are critical to setting the agenda for change and getting the ball rolling. Communication has to be of and from the heart of the organisation and if no obvious centre exists to play that role, one will have to be created. This could be a temporary arrangement for the purpose of the integration of the business strategy. Those at the core of this activity could include the CEO, HR director, head of communication, and perhaps consulting support. The aim is to develop a structured approach based on stakeholder needs to deal with information, issues and concerns with the ultimate aim of accelerating change.

Key responsibilities of this central task force are to define the strategy, identify stakeholder groups, determine the most effective channels for communication and feedback, and agree on measures for success. The task force is then responsible for driving the process, shaping core messages and obtaining senior management buy-in. Working with others, they develop materials, coach local "champions," and manage distribution and timing as well as feedback processes. The feedback mechanism helps identify issues and concerns for which the group can plan their response and action plans. Throughout the process, they will monitor communication effectiveness and achievement against objectives.

During this time, communication has to take account of and deal with the Seven Cs of Change™:

1. Context: Why are we doing this? What will happen if we don't do it? What are the competitive pressures? What are our customers telling us?
2. Clarity: What is our vision for the future? What will it be like if we achieve it? What will I experience in this new state?
3. Control: Who owns this initiative? Is management fully invested? How is progress being measured? Who is keeping us on track?

4. Calendar: What's the timescale for this initiative? When will it be over? What milestones should I be able to identify?

5. Contribution: What do I need to do differently? Do I need to do different things? How will my performance be measured?

6. Conditions: How will I be rewarded for adopting the new ways of working? How will my job change? What support mechanisms are in place?

7. Consideration: What if I have difficulty adapting? What will happen if my pace of change is slower than normal?

These issues may not be dealt with in this particular order, and people will have different questions and concerns, but they all have to be covered if people are to cooperate and play their part. People may resist change, but they will embrace progress when it is properly framed.

In a study done by Mercer Management Consulting (1995) on companies who went through a slow transition process versus a fast transition process, some remarkable differences were found. In all cases, fast transition companies outperformed their counterparts significantly. In terms of business performance, they were ahead in market share, stock price, productivity, operating expenses, investment and technical progress. In terms of favourable attitudes and behaviours, they were ahead in innovation, product focus, energy and commitment, morale, initiative, clarity of direction, and customer focus.

Working quickly and with a clear focus on actions and behaviours, and using a communication management matrix as a guide, this is a low-risk investment with great potential returns.

Elements of change

There are five vital elements in constructing an effective change campaign:

1. Clear vision
2. Pressure for change
3. Capacity for change
4. Actionable first steps
5. Measureable progress tied to business outcomes

All five have to be in place. Without a clear vision, the change effort will falter. No pressure to change means that change initiatives will stay at the bottom of the in-tray. No capacity to change will lead to anxiety and frustration, while the absence of actionable first steps will lead to haphazard attempts and loss of direction. Measuring progress helps people understand where they are on the change journey.

Developing the Vision

- Develop a compelling vision of the future that "pulls" the change initiative along
- Use as many means as possible to communicate the vision—cultural, structural and systematic (formal, informal and interpersonal)
- Ensure visible involvement from top management—both time and resources
- Establish role models to champion the new behaviours, linking them with the values
- Articulate a clear picture of the organisation of the future
- Be clear about the type of change that is required

Create the Pressure to Change

- Communicate or lead people to discover market realities
- Highlight actual or perceived potential crises; drive people out of their comfort zones; create "burning platforms."
- Highlight potential attractive opportunities

- Clearly identify the gap between the actual and desired state
- Feed in ongoing external intelligence; connect with the marketplace
- Conduct stakeholder analysis and target messages

Create the Capacity for Change

- Surface and understand the cultural issues, including those that are taken for granted and seldom, if ever, questioned
- Manage people through the change process
- Pre-empt resistance; understand what people have to gain or lose
- Encourage risk-taking; destroy any blame culture
- Develop the necessary skill base
- Align individual performance with the business strategy
- Focus the cause and context for change in the marketplace
- Facilitate bottom-up entrepreneurship

Actionable First Steps

- Plan for short-term actions that will deliver visible wins
- Recognise and reward employees involved in these wins
- Set clearly defined objectives and responsibilities
- Articulate what is necessary to complete the change journey
- Consolidate the process as you go

Measure progress in business outcomes

- Identify the measures that demonstrate progress against the objectives you set at the start of the journey

Sometimes it gets tough

RBS Group started life humbly in Edinburgh, Scotland set up by Royal Charter granted in 1727 by King George I as The Royal Bank of Scotland. In 1728 it granted the world's first overdraft to an Edinburgh merchant, William Hog. Hog had found that his creditors required to be paid before he was able to collect from his debtors and so the Bank agreed that he could temporarily take more money from his account than he had in it. Hog became the world's first recipient of a cash credit.

Fast forward to recent times: if only it was that simple now. RBS Group had grown by acquisition on the realisation that critical mass was a prerequisite to compete in what was rapidly becoming a global marketplace. It had grown its Citizens franchise over a ten year period and subsequently acquired Charter One in the US; NatWest in the biggest takeover in British banking history; and in 2007 the Dutch banking group ABN AMRO in what was the world's biggest banking deal (£48bn). By then it has 170,000 people in fifty countries.

But something insidious was happening. RBS got caught up in the bust of the American housing market, which was fuelled by the availability of easy money through risky subprime loans.

Many mortgage-backed securities were bundled into structured products and sold on within the financial community. As preferential loan rates expired and interest payments increased, people started to default on their repayments. Credit became much harder to get, banks were cautious about lending to each other—and then came the tipping point.

In RBS, employees could see that something was happening. The share price, which had stood at 6.90GBP* in early 2007, dropped steadily to 3.63GBP by April 2008; when the bank launched a rights issue—the opportunity for existing shareholders to acquire new stock at an agreed-upon price. [*At the time of writing 1.00 GBP = 1.60 USD]

Despite this, the share price continued to fall because of the global banking crisis and increasing worries over RBS' liquidity.

Despite the financial turmoil, RBS decided to go ahead with its annual employee survey in September 2008. The worst news came during the last week of the survey when the U.K. government had to rescue the bank from collapse. When the results were analysed, there was a significant worsening in employee opinion between completions at the start and the end of the survey. Over the years, employees had become more and more positive about RBS as an employer (the bank was ranked in the Towers Perrin-ISR high performing companies' index). They were now in a very different situation.

Most employees were also shareholders, and they had witnessed their "nest-eggs" disappearing and any options going well under water. They clearly blamed leadership for the situation and were shocked, angry, confused and let down.

The blame wasn't laid at the door of immediate supervisors but that of the most senior leaders, notably Sir Fred Goodwin, chief executive, who had taken the bank on the acquisition trail culminating with ABN AMRO, which had a lot of toxic debt. Communication during the year had been factual and honest but reactive. Many in communication, who were used to telling good news stories for so long, hadn't the experience of dealing with bad news so they too had a steep learning curve.

In October of 2008, Sir Fred Goodwin resigned as a consequence of the bank having been bailed out by the British tax payer—and the share price languished at 0.64GBP. It eventually fell as far as 0.10GBP.

Roughly 169,650 of the 170,000 employed by RBS Group had nothing to do with the situation in which the bank found itself. So you can imagine how the vast majority of employees felt.

Buoyed by government money and new Chief Executive Stephen Hester, the bank set about restructuring. Communication now had to be proactive, transparent and honest. Some businesses were sold, there were some redundancies and the transition was speedy. The chief executive led from the front, getting out of his office and visiting employees. The most senior managers and middle managers were given the information and tools to cascade developments to their people. All channels and media were mobilized: Face-to-face meetings, audio calls, the intranet and social media all played a part. The volume of communication had certainly been turned up but so too had the quality and content. The CEO and the group human resources director also posted regular updates, which were positively received.

RBS Group, at the time of writing, had 150,000 people in 30 countries because of its divestments. The 2010 employee survey showed a remarkable improvement in employee opinion and attitude, not just against previous results but higher than the market average for the sector, particularly in the areas of leadership and communication.

7. THE JOURNEY STARTS WITH A SINGLE STEP

Executives can usually understand the systemic nature of engagement when they encounter it for the first time, and they probably subscribe to it in principle. One of the reasons that it is not practised most likely lies in the seeming enormity and longevity of the task. It probably ends up in the "too difficult" box, and a silver bullet is sought.

The journey needn't be onerous, but it must be faithfully followed through. There are three ways to do so:

- Clean slate
- Pressing issue
- Organisational diagnostic

Clean slate

A clean slate will rarely occur as it means almost starting from scratch and building the desired organisation from the ground up. General Motors took just such an opportunity in 1990 with the setup of its Saturn plant in Spring Hill, Tennessee.

This was a novel attempt to break away from the confrontational labour relations style and inflexible practices that had long plagued the U.S. car industry. At Saturn, GM and the United Auto Workers Union signed a separate contract that gave workers a voice in designing vehicles, picking suppliers and planning production processes. In exchange for a no-layoffs clause, workers agreed to have 20 percent of their compensation tied to productivity goals and agreed to a flexible workplace with relatively few job classifications, where they were cross-trained to perform a variety of tasks. This was a process built on trust and respect.

While this was a revelation at GM, the car brand itself struggled, and never became a sales leader, but it did have an enthusiastic and almost cult-like following. Because of the lack of sales volume and the difficulties engulfing the motor industry, GM absorbed Saturn into its companywide Global Manufacturing System in 2004, and Saturn workers now have the same contract as the rest of GM's workforce. However, Saturn's practices were reverse engineered into GM where people witnessed more flexibility, collegiality, and team-working.

Pressing issue

Pressing issues are much more commonplace than the clean slate. Like the Clydesdale Bank in the earlier example, we need to find out what the real causes of the problem are, deal with them and then most important, support them elsewhere in the system. It can be dangerous to assume that because you have dealt with the presenting issue, the box can be ticked.

Babcock Marine, part of Babcock International, is the major support partner to the Royal Navy. The division also provides services to customers in the civil marine markets and has one of the largest naval design capabilities in the U.K. It is the sole provider of support to the Royal Navy's submarine fleet at HMNB Clyde and HMNB Devonport in Plymouth.

HMNB Clyde (Her Majesty's Naval Base) presented with a communication issue. Management felt that there wasn't enough understanding or buy-in from employees for the business objectives or vision for the future. A survey and focus groups allowed them to focus on a number of key issues, and a programme was put in place to deal with the findings. This involved facilitating a discussion with senior managers about their engagement philosophy and strategy (like the one described in Chapter 6) and then putting in place a planning cycle for communication and involvement activities. All directors, senior managers and supervisors attended sessions on employee engagement; engagement in turn formed part of the performance management system for managers and played a significant part in their bonus calculation.

In order to increase levels of engagement, the company decided to design a narrative graphic outlining the organisation's journey, mission and vision that would be relevant to everyone irrespective of their position in the organisation. The graphic stimulated discussion of the business goals and values, change factors and achievements to date, as well as hopes for the future. It allowed all staff to feel ownership of the company's vision and the strategy required to achieve it. Following this exercise, management created a business plan that was written in plain language so that everyone would be able to visualise exactly how and where they contributed to the success of the organisation. Managers and team leaders were challenged individually to identify which high-level objectives were most pertinent to their teams and in what ways. A number of departments created their own mini business plan to contextualize objectives for their people at a local level.

Babcock Marine was cited as an exemplar of employee engagement in the MacLeod Report (2009), which stated that,

"Tangible benefits that have been attributed, at least in part, to various engagement activities include a reduction of 30 per cent in sickness absence between 2005 & 2009 and a 50 per cent reduction in reportable accidents from 18 to nine between 2007/08 and 2008/09. Project performance has significantly improved, resulting in overall project performance going from a 48 per cent overrun to less than three per cent" (pp. 76-77).

Organisational diagnostic

You can learn a lot about an organisation by walking about, talking to people, listening to them and observing how they act. You can get to the emotion, perception, and beliefs and feelings around issues by running focus groups. If you want hard numbers (and senior executives like hard numbers) on engagement and its drivers, you will have to conduct a survey.

Surveying is like pulling the pin on a hand grenade; if you don't do something with it, it will harm you. Many companies conduct surveys, don't like what they find and bury the results. And many organisations, faced with the prospect of counselling employee opinion, shy away from it because they fear what they might find. This is like refusing to go to the doctor when you suspect a malady in case she finds you have a serious illness. It is always better to know for certain and deal with the findings.

Benchmarking survey results against other organisations is another distraction. It is time-consuming, relatively expensive and produces no real benefit in this context. Exactly the same questions would have to be asked of the same sort of people in the same industry to get close to a benchmark. But even then, the data could not account for a different cultural environment or climate. Visionary companies don't worry about anyone else; they seek to better themselves by charting where they are versus where they want to be. Surveys therefore have to be focused, pragmatic, and produce actionable results. Too many survey instruments ask questions about satisfaction and advocacy and call positive findings "engagement" when they are patently not. Some broad-based workplace survey data may be useful as a guide but don't sweat over it.

Dunfermline Building Society (DBS) used an annual survey to drive its people strategy. During 2004-2007, Dunfermline had just over 500 staff operating in the head office and in 34 branches. In a competitive market with much bigger players, Dunfermline's differentiator was customer service. Until 2004, the organisation had counselled employee opinion through surveys, examining attitudes and satisfaction. The results were generally good, and overall satisfaction was high, but there was recognition that in the highly competitive market place in which they were operating, they had to be more rigorous in their approach. Alan Mitchell, the general manager in charge of the people strategy appointed Maryann Handy as the business manager in charge of employee engagement. Maryann explained:

"We are in the high street competing against bigger firms. From a product perspective, we obviously have to be competitive but if our people are not engaged, that will not translate well at the point of contact with the customer. We have recognised that our people are what give us our point of difference and we need to build on that."

They decided to use a proprietary research instrument (the Q^4 Profiler™) that examines the employment experience in 12 dimensions:

1. Recruitment and induction
2. Vision and mission
3. Values
4. Organisation design
5. Leadership and management
6. Performance management
7. Reward and recognition
8. Communication and involvement
9. Learning and development
10. Work-life balance
11. Reputation
12. Employer Brand

It also examines factors of attraction, motivation and retention, and from the responses to identified questions, can produce data on advocacy, trust, alignment, commitment and engagement.

Significantly, the executive team can also complete the questionnaire from their perspective, which provides a useful starting point for dialogue on their view of policies and processes as well as the similarities and differences from employee responses. DBS was particularly brave in that it also published results for the executive team split by geography and reporting line. Each member of the executive team could clearly see where the issues were on his or her watch.

It is not unusual to look first at the alignment, commitment and engagement scores and then revert to the main dimensions to find out what is driving the result. In this context, the combination of alignment and commitment is the engagement score, which can be displayed on a matrix (Fig 7.1).

Alignment and Commitment Matrix

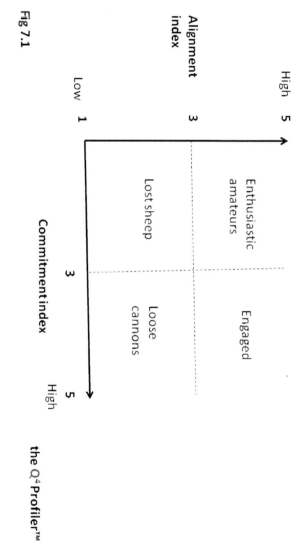

Fig 7.1

the Q⁴ Profiler™

All questions comprising alignment and commitment are scored on a Likert scale. The final score is the weighted mean score for that section. A score of over 3.0 in alignment and commitment will place the overall employee population in the engaged quadrant; however, position in that quadrant is significant.

The other three quadrants in the model are as follows:

Enthusiastic amateurs are people who are aligned with organisational goals; they understand them and concur with them, but they are probably not going to go too far out of their way to help achieve them. They stay in their comfort zone and are likely to be satisfied but are obviously not engaged.

Loose canons are committed but not aligned. They may be committed to their job or their own agenda but not necessarily to working in support of organisational objectives. They could be demonstrating misplaced discretionary effort.

Lost sheep are neither aligned nor committed. They may be confused or floundering, and some may be looking for a way out.

In 2004, DBS scored 3.62 on alignment and 3.28 on commitment from a 78 percent response. Digging into the data, it was found that people were on-side with vision, values and business objectives; they felt the Society had a strong reputation and that it provided good products and services. Areas of concern included a perception that reward was not on market and that the reward policy may not be fair. Few could see the link between performance and reward, and they weren't convinced that DBS could attract and retain talent. There was also a perceived disconnect between the head office and the branches.

The results were discussed with staff in their regular communication forums, and issues raised there went directly to the executive team. Over the coming months, DBS tackled a number of issues:

- Recruitment and induction: Managers were given additional training in interview skills, and less experienced managers were given a "buddy." Employer brand values were introduced into the recruitment process. Head office and branch induction began to overlap by one day, and a tour of the head office was included for branch employees. The employer brand was made more explicit at induction, and a member of the executive team joined inductees for lunch.

- Performance management: Performance management and personal development processes were reviewed. The performance management assessment was reduced from an 18-point scale to a four-point scale, and managers received training on how to handle underperformance.
- Rewards: Executive pay was reviewed, and all jobs were benchmarked against the market. Graphic explanations highlighted the links between organisational success and pay scales. The company instituted improved transparency on reward policy and market and individual relativities.
- Leadership and management: Dunfermline instigated a learning and development programme for managers at all levels, including a responsibility to communicate business information to all employees.

This was typical of the way the organisation responded to survey results each year. They clearly stated the findings, warts and all, and then explained what they would do about them, involving staff in the process.

In 2005 DBS again scored 3.62 on alignment, but commitment dropped to 3.18, and the response rate also dropped to 73 percent. This was not the result that had been expected. Despite their efforts over the previous months, reward was still being flagged as an issue as was the perceived ability to recruit talent. More significant, however, was people's disaffection over Project Destiny, an IT initiative designed to link all of the Society's disparate systems together. It was behind schedule and experiencing operational difficulties, which fostered a growing sense of frustration and cynicism among staff who had been promised an imminent improvement in IT provision. DBS developed a competency-based recruitment process and looked again at pay and benefits compared to the market as well as monitoring attrition on a monthly basis.

In 2006 the scores were alignment: 3.65 and commitment: 3.39. At last, commitment had recovered to a position above where it had been two years earlier, and alignment was up slightly as well. The big picture was very positive, and participation in the survey increased (84 percent). Finally, reward was seen as less of an issue as scores in that dimension increased; up too were scores on learning and development and advocacy. (Reminder: advocacy is often taken as a positive sign of engagement. On its own, it is not. People could simply be satisfied; it has to be considered alongside other factors.)

Having now completed three survey cycles, consistent upward and downward trends were examined and, over the piece, there were a few in each category. Significantly, the upward trends included values influencing day-to-day behaviours, clarity on business goals, reward and recognition, learning and development, and performance management. Some negative trends were on vision, organisation design, and Project Destiny. Over the coming months, the Society focused on reaffirming the positive trends and sought to address the negative ones.

In 2007 alignment was up to 3.82 and commitment up to 3.57. These shifts may not seem like a lot, but in evidence for the MacLeod Report (2009), Standard Chartered Bank reported that in 2007 they found that branches with a statistically significant increase in levels of employee engagement (0.2 or more on a scale of five) had a 16 percent higher profit margin growth than branches with decreased levels of employee engagement.

DBS was about to discover similar benefits. As seen in figure 7.2, from 2004 to 2007 an already high customer satisfaction score had increased, but, more significantly (as seen in figure 7.3) profits increased 51 percent, and member value (DBS is a mutual) rose by 70 percent. In that environment, only the engagement of people can explain these results. In 2007, 84.6 percent of DBS employees were engaged (in Fig 7.4 each dot is a person and the darker areas clusters of people).

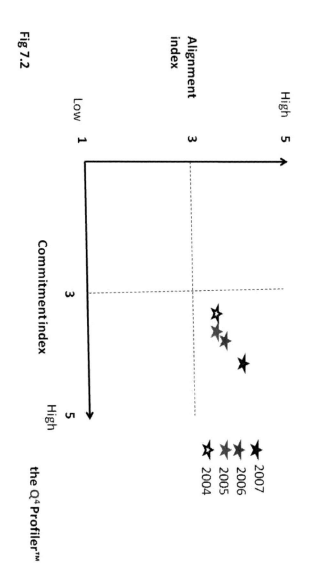

Alignment and Commitment Matrix

Fig 7.2

the Q⁴ Profiler™

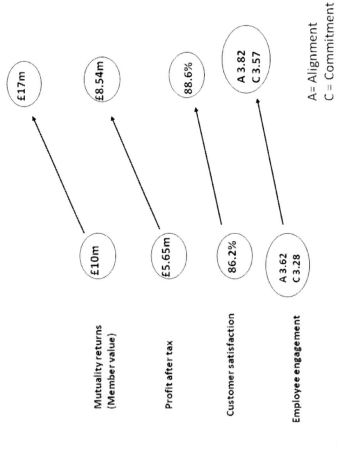

Links to performance at DBS

Mutuality returns (Member value): £10m → £17m

Profit after tax: £5.65m → £8.54m

Customer satisfaction: 86.2% → 88.6%

Employee engagement: A 3.62 C 3.28 → A 3.82 C 3.57

A = Alignment
C = Commitment

Fig 7.3

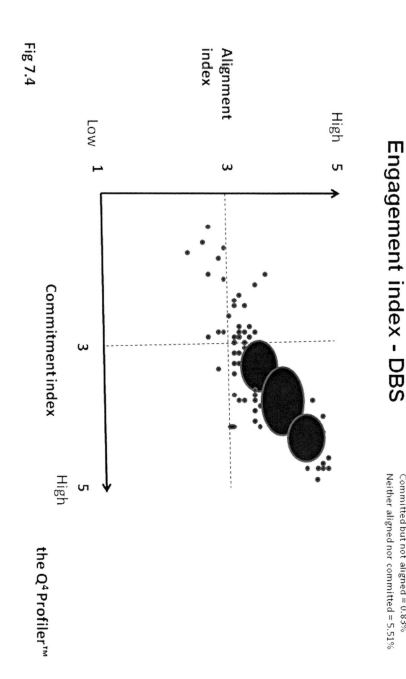

Engagement index - DBS

Fig 7.4

the Q⁴ Profiler™

Engaged = 84.57%
Aligned but not committed = 9.09%
Committed but not aligned = 0.83%
Neither aligned nor committed = 5.51%

In 2008, the HR team at Dunfermline won the HR Team of the Year Award at the HR Network National Awards. In praising his team (reward, learning and development, and engagement managers) Alan Mitchell commented, "They totally bought into the engagement concept from the off and took everyone in the business with them; the annual survey explicated the issues and brought transparency and focus to our people strategy."

2008 was also the year of the financial crisis and, being a relatively small player with a diverse business structure and a not insignificant commercial property book; DBS was assimilated into the Nationwide Building Society; however the brand, the branches and the ethos remain.

Holding up a mirror

Conducting a survey effectively means holding up a mirror to the organisation and reflecting current attitudes, perceptions and behaviours. To understand engagement it has to be comprehensive and robust, for which there is no space here, but to kick-start your thinking, here are some questions for you to consider about your organisation.

1. To what extent do your people understand your mission and business strategy?
2. Do people know what they can do to help achieve your mission and business strategy?
3. Do your values transparently influence policies and behaviours?
4. Do your leaders "live" the values?
5. Do employees know what is expected of them in their jobs?
6. Are there clear links between individual objectives, departmental objectives and organisational goals?
7. Do your practices reinforce the importance of customers to the organisation?
8. Will adherence to values (or not) influence an individual's prospects?
9. Are your people committed to your objectives?

10. Do people demonstrate "extra-role" behaviour?
11. To what extent do your leaders inspire trust?
12. Do employees have confidence in the decisions made by leaders?
13. To what extent can people influence their objectives?
14. Are there clear links between performance and reward?
15. Are people encouraged to manage their own development?
16. Does the organisation support professional development opportunities?
17. Is communication open, honest and timely?
18. Do people get involved in decisions that might affect them?
19. Are people given enough information to understand the context for business decisions?
20. Would your employees recommend your organisation as a place to work?

8. REFRAMING ENGAGEMENT

A Watson Wyatt study of 115 companies suggested that a company with highly engaged employees achieves a financial performance four times greater than companies with poor engagement. In addition, the highly engaged are more than twice as likely to be top performers—almost 60 percent of them exceed or far exceed expectations for performance. Moreover, the highly engaged missed 43 percent fewer days of work due to illness. (*Continuous Engagement: The Key to Unlocking the Value of Your People During Tough Times, Work Europe Survey, Watson Wyatt—2008-2009.*)

Gallup has also found that engagement levels can be predictors of sickness absence, with more highly engaged employees taking an average of 2.7 days per year, compared with disengaged employees taking an average of 6.2 days per year (Harter, Schmidt, Kilham, Asplund, 2006).

Hewitt (2004) reported that companies with a greater than 10 percent profit growth had 39 percent more engaged employees and 45 percent fewer disengaged employees than those with less than 10 percent growth.

Development Dimension International (DDI) reported that in a Fortune 100 manufacturing company, turnover in low engagement teams averaged 14.5 percent compared with 4.8 percent in high engagement teams. Absenteeism in low engagement teams hovered around 8 percent, but was down to 4.1 percent in high engagement teams. Quality errors were significantly higher for poorly engaged teams. (Wellins, R. S., Bernthal, P. & Phelps, M (2005). 'Employee engagement: the key to realising competitive advantage', DDI and at: http://www.ddiworld.com/pdf/ddi_employeeengagement_mg.pdf)

Organisations with high employee engagement out-perform those with lower engagement on a Total Returns to Shareholders (TRS) basis by almost 100 percent (Watson Wyatt HCI, 2002). Significantly, when times are tough, as they have been over the past few years, TRS is down because the markets are down, but the highly engaged companies are still outstripping the market.

In short, engaged employees perform; therefore, engagement is a business imperative.

Creating a sustainable differentiator

As we can see from the above, engaged employees tend to do the right things with enough frequency and in the right way, that performance, however it is measured, is impacted positively. Strong performance, goal achievement and organisational success can all be results of an engagement focus. While this will help the organisation develop year over year, how can this be utilized to create competitive advantage?

The traditional battleground for seeking an advantage over the competition includes the products and services an organisation produces, in terms of design, function and quality; pricing; distribution; marketing and advertising; IT systems; and support. Advantage gained in this way is only sustainable if the cost of entry is too high for aspiring competitors. The problem is that most of these differentiating attributes can be copied or acquired. The time lag between innovation and imitation can now be measured in weeks rather than years. So where does sustainable competitive advantage come from?

According to Terry R. Bacon, writing in the Lore International Institute White Paper Series in 2002, organisations should differentiate through behaviour. Calling this process Behavioural Differentiation, Bacon (2002) explains,

"Behavioural differentiation is difficult to copy because it requires more skill and will than many companies have—even when they know what they are doing. There is a huge gap between knowing how to behave and behaving that way consistently" (p. 2).

Working alongside other attributes of the organisation, these behaviours have to be perceived as differentiating. They could be unique to your organisation, or you may just be much better at them than competitors. Customers will see this, and if they perceive value in these behaviours, they will enhance the customer experience.

There are, Bacon says, four key differentiating behaviours:

1. Operational behaviours: These reflect the way the business operates; they are standard operating procedures (SOPs) if you like. While most will be transactional, they are constructed with differentiation from competitors in mind. This is an example of state engagement.
2. Interpersonal behaviour: This is about the way staff interacts personally with customers; therefore, it has more to do with the attitude and personality of these people rather than something that can be operationalised. Recruiting the right people for these roles is critical, as is reinforcing and rewarding the desired behaviours. Customers can see through the inauthentic, "Have a nice day" approach. This is trait engagement at work.
3. Exceptional behaviour: This is people taking on extra-role responsibilities to work in the customer's interest and exceed their expectations. It is important, therefore, that staff feel they have the freedom to work on their initiative, even outside standard operating procedures, if it benefits the customer and enhances the image and reputation of the business. This is behavioural engagement as described in Chapter 2.
4. Symbolic behaviour: These behaviours reflect and endorse your key product and service offerings. Your organisation is walking the talk and ensuring that there are clear linkages between the rhetoric of its marketing and the reality of dealing with it.

While in Bacon's work the focus is on external customer relationships, there is no reason why in an engaged workforce these principles do not apply internally with colleagues and externally with suppliers and other communities of interest. An article by Harter et al in the *Harvard Business Review* (2002) found that customer and employee engagement augment each other at the local level, creating an opportunity for accelerated improvement and growth of overall financial performance. Analysis of the performance of 1,979 business units in 10 companies revealed that those units that scored above the median on both employee and customer engagement were on average 3.4 times more effective financially (in terms of total sales and revenue performance to target, and year over year gain in sales and revenue) than units in the bottom half of both measures.

For this approach to work, three key components (Fig 8.1) must be present: leadership, culture, and process. Leadership must be fully invested, involved in and committed to the process. Leaders have to model the desired behaviours consistently and encourage others to do the same, thus giving people a degree of flexibility in expressing themselves as they master new ways of working. Culturally, the core purpose and core values must influence the key operational processes and desired behavioural outcomes; this must be further enhanced and supported by the organisation structure and people management policies and processes, including recruitment and induction, organisation design, communication, performance management, total rewards, and learning and development. No doubt this is beginning to feel familiar; we're back in the experiential engagement system construct (Fig 5.2)

What you create inside the organisation will have a positive impact outside the organisation (Fig 8.2). The employment experience conditions the desired behaviours to the benefit of customers, suppliers and, to a lesser but still important extent, communities and shareholders. The first-party experience influences the third-party experience at the point of contact. That intersection is the source of sustainable competitive advantage; thus, how your external stakeholders experience your organisation through your people is critical.

Key requirements

Leadership

Buy-in
Commitment
Involvement
Role-modelling
Consistency

Culture

Values influencing
processes and
behaviours

Process

Recruitment
Organisation design
Communication
Performance
management
Total reward
Learning &
development

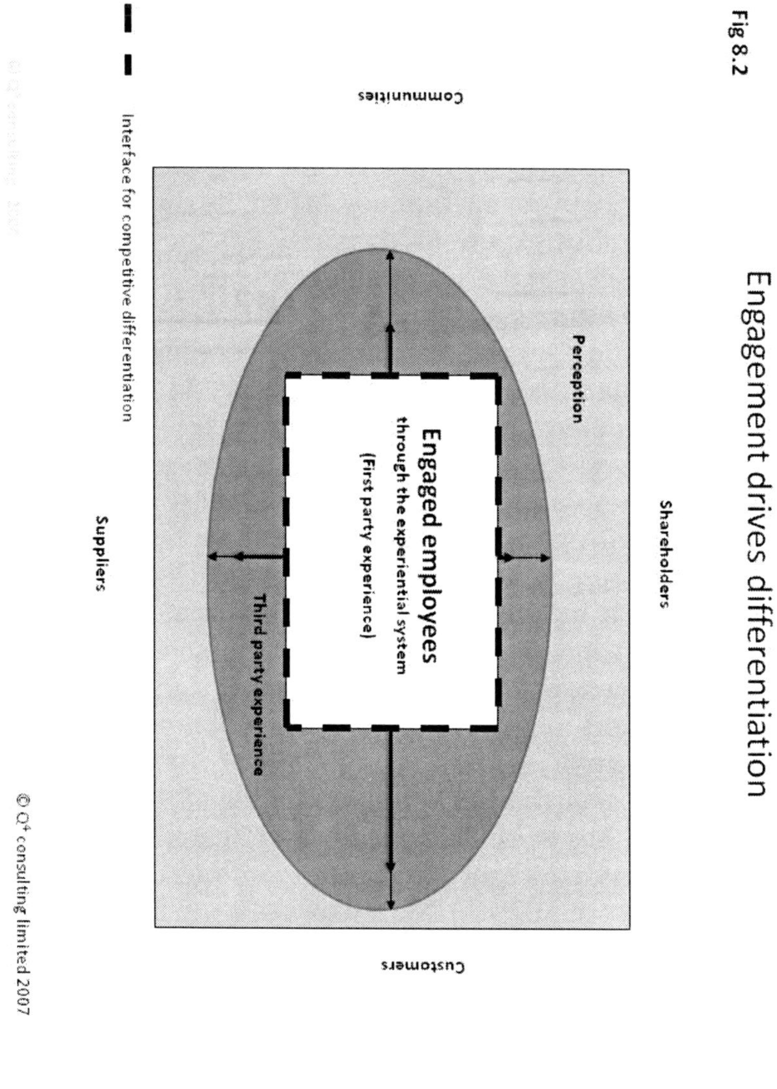

Fig 8.2

Engagement drives differentiation

Communities

Perception

Shareholders

Engaged employees
through the experiential system
(First party experience)

Third party experience

Suppliers

Customers

Interface for competitive differentiation

© Q⁴ consulting limited 2007

Driving performance

One of the top three reasons that CEOs assiduously nurture their organisation's reputation is its ability to attract talent. Some of that energy has to translate into ensuring that talent is appropriately engaged. The CEO makes promises to customers and stakeholders that rely for their fulfilment on employees. Fulfilling these promises enhances reputation and helps attract investment and talented employees. The CEO therefore has to be totally invested in engagement—not just the rhetoric but the holistic reality of the experiential system. It is the number one business imperative in the knowledge economy, and without it, there will be no future success.

There is a small but growing number of organisations keen to use engagement as a performance metric, and this will be used in part to determine management bonuses at all levels. If institutional investors see the benefit of an engaged workforce, there will be more pressure on CEOs to adopt that approach. If the CEO's performance bonus is in part based on workforce engagement, you can be sure that leaders at all levels in the organisation will be similarly assessed. This may also lead to the demise of short-termism and focussing solely on profit. When profit becomes the main focus there is a danger of failing in strategic intent—or failing period. We all know this to our cost in recent years!

No one expects the CEO to spend a lot of working time on this issue; it has to be delegated but delegated with a clear strategy and mandate aligned to the organisation's core ideology (the engagement manifesto). Most likely, this will fall to human resources; after all they have many of the levers to pull, and they will be supported by internal communication wherever that sits in the organisation.

But engagement is everyone's responsibility and it goes all the way to first-line supervision. There is no point in lumbering someone with engagement in their role title: head of people and engagement, head of human resources and engagement, head of communication and engagement, or worse, head of employee engagement.

Why? Four reasons:

- First, others will think that it is that person's responsibility;
- Second, no single job role has the influence to create engagement in a workforce, especially if it is two or three steps removed from the CEO in the organisational hierarchy;
- Third, engagement will be consigned to tactical interventions or initiatives, which may provide short-term benefit but which cannot drive sustainable competitive advantage;
- Fourth, it may have influence or control over process, but it can't have control over the employment experience. And that's what drives engagement—or not.

We all have to raise our game and indulge in some joined-up strategic thinking if our engagement practices are to deliver on a sustainable basis. It requires policy makers, functional heads, and operational management working collaboratively and cohesively to drive the desired outcomes. Engagement won't be effected by an individual, but it could be affected by an individual. Engagement is powerful, but it is also fragile. Many years of good work can be ruined by a bad decision, poor execution or an ill-advised comment.

What's in a name?

And so what about engagement? How do we ensure that when we use the term, hear it, and especially if we want to measure it; ensure that we understand what it means? One just has to read the comments on LinkedIn groups on the subject to see that 90 percent of contributors are looking through the wrong end of the telescope—exclusively tactical and often misdirected. Is there a difference between engaging with employees and employee engagement? Yes, and it is a significant one. The former, which includes communication and involvement activities, can influence performance positively and can contribute significantly to employee engagement. However, practised on its own, the impact is unlikely to be sustainable; other parts of the experiential system have to be aligned and supportive.

Is the former 'engagement' and the latter 'Engagement'?

No. The former is 'putting old wine in new bottles' as some academics have suggested—it is actually communication as described in Chapter 6. The latter is engagement as defined in Chapter 2, and described contextually, systemically, and experientially in subsequent chapters. Mostly engagement has been treated as a synonym for communication and involvement. As if communication wasn't an important enough discipline! This author has also been guilty of that in the past, but beware of the implied promise that 'engagement' carries.

If we have to delineate, think of the systemic approach described here as macro-engagement; and all the individual strategies or tactical interventions around leadership, performance, reward, communication, learning and development and so on; as micro-engagement activities. These areas of focus can all contribute to overall workforce engagement. And only if they are properly aligned, congruent and mutually supportive, will they produce a whole that is greater than the sum of its parts. Ideally, the macro-engagement philosophy will drive and sustain everything else.

Engagement is not a strategy. It sits alongside core purpose and core values; it should be part of your core ideology, not an ex-works retro-fit. It is a way of being; a practical philosophy. It is memetic, a fundamental guiding principle that informs your policies, processes and behaviours.

If we allow the engagement game to be played by the wrong rules then it will wither and die as just another management fad that failed to deliver on its promise. Maybe we can't change what it's called but we can change the rules. And if enough of us hold this to be true it can become true for everyone.

"When we dream alone, it is only a dream. When we dream together, it is no longer a dream, but the beginning of reality."

Brazilian proverb

The following are some rules of engagement to keep in mind:

1. Be clear about what you mean by engagement.
2. Ensure senior executives are fully invested in it.
3. Clarify how you will measure engagement and identify the contributing factors.
4. Ensure that everything you do supports your core purpose and values.
5. Where action is required, acknowledge that a single intervention is unlikely to be successful. It will have to be supported elsewhere in the system.
6. Keep the lines of communication and consultation open.
7. Wherever you sit in the organisation, collaborate with your colleagues. They may have more useful levers to pull than you do (see No. 5).
8. Engagement is not an event; it is a never-ending journey.
9. Look for and measure the impact of engagement in your business results and link them to objectives.
10. Recognise, reward, celebrate and reinforce what you are doing well—and keep doing it.

Following the engagement manifesto can enable your organisation to attract, truly engage and retain talent. Your engaged and behaviourally differentiated employees will delight your customers, who will provide you with repeat business and referrals, and the resultant financials will keep your shareholders happy.

Your employees, as well as being engaged, will feel fulfilled and satisfied. You have created the essence of your employer brand; no other effort is necessary in its pursuit, just decide with your advertising agency how it should be articulated and promoted. You will have created a sustainable competitive advantage and in the process enhanced your reputation.

It is a virtuous circle—or wheel!

ACKNOWLEDGEMENTS

I must thank all the clients over the years who have allowed me to ply my trade and learn in the process. A particular mention must go to the employees of those client companies, for it is they who provide most of the learning.

My colleagues at The Ghost Partnership, John Nicholson and Bill Mitchell, encouraged me in this endeavour, read manuscripts and provided valuable counsel. Sandra Crozier reviewed the content from an educational perspective and nailed my feet firmly to the floor.

Thanks also to Graeme Dalziel, CEO; Alan Mitchell, general manager people strategy; Maryann Handy, business manager, Dunfermline Building Society;

Neil Roden, group human resources director, RBS Group; Martin Rettie, region manager—corporate total rewards, Transocean.

I have been fortunate to work with some gifted and inspirational people over the years, and you can't experience that without taking on board sound philosophies, good ideas, and excellent practice almost by osmosis. There have been many, but I would like to name-check a few: Valerie Brandvik, Brendan McCann, Nick Prentice, Angela Sinickas, Clive Chajet, Dave Johnston and Roger D'Aprix.

I thank Michael Michalko for allowing me to use his tale of "The Five Monkeys." It served its purpose perfectly. All other sources are listed in the references section.

REFERENCES

Argyris, C. (1960). *Understanding organisational behaviour.* Homewood, Illinois: Dorsey Press.

Armstrong, M. & **Baron**, A. (1998). *Performance management: The new realities.* London: Institute of Personnel and Development.

Bacon, T. R., & **Pugh**, D. G. (2003). *Winning behaviour: What the smartest, most successful companies do differently.* New York City: American Management Association.

Baron, A (2006) In T. L. Gillis (Ed.), *The IABC handbook of organisational communication.*, San Francisco, Jossey Bass

Bond, M. H. (2002). Reclaiming the individual from Hofstede's ecological analysis—a 20-year odyssey: Comment on Oyserman et al. *Psychological Bulletin, 128* No1 pp.73-77.

Brown, A. (1995). *Organisational culture.* Pitman Press, London, p.2.

Collins, J., & **Porras**, J. I. (1994). *Built to last: Successful habits of visionary companies.* Random House. London

Cropanzano, R., & **Mitchell**, M. S. (2005). Social exchange theory: An interdisciplinary review. *Journal of Management, Vol 31/6, pp* 874-900.

Crozier, R. A. (2006). Employer branding. In S. Reddy (Ed.), *Integrating HR and marketing strategies.* (93-107) The ICFAI University press, Hyderabad

Crozier, R. A. (2006). Internal branding: Employer branding. In T. L. Gillis (Ed.), *The IABC handbook of organisational communication.* (268-279). San Francisco: Jossey-Bass.

Crozier, R. A. (1998). *Total employment relationship management.* Conference proceedings, Fairleigh Dickinson University. New Jersey

Deal, T., & **Kennedy**, A. (1982). *Corporate cultures: The rites and rituals of corporate life.* Addison-Wesley. London.

Erikson, T. J. (2005). Testimony submitted before the U.S. Senate Committee on Health, Education, Labor and Pensions, May 26.

Fombrun, C. (1996). *Reputation: Realizing value from the corporate image.* Boston: Harvard Business School Press.

Gonzalez-Roma, V., **Schaufeli**, W. B., **Bakker**, A. B., & **Lloret**, S. (2006). Burnout and work engagement: Independent factors or opposite poles? *Journal of Vocational Behaviour, 68/*1 pp165-174.

Handy, C. B. (1978). *The fods of management.* London: Penguin.

Handy, C. B. (1985). *Understanding organisations.* London: Penguin.

Harrison, R. (1972). Understanding your organisation's character. *Harvard Business Review,* May-June 1972, Vol 50 May/June pp.119-128.

Harter, J. K., **Schmidt**, F. L., & **Hayes**, T. L. (2002). Business unit level relationship between employee satisfaction, employee engagement, and business outcomes: A meta-analysis. *Journal of Applied Psychology, 87/*2 268-279.

Herzberg, F. (1962). *Work and the nature of man.* New York, Thomas Y Crowell Co

Hofstede, G., **Hofstede**, G. J., & **Minkov**, M. (2010). *Culture and organisations: software for the mind.* New York City: McGraw Hill.

Kanter, R. M. (1989). *When giants learn to dance: Mastering the challenge of strategy, management and careers in the 1990s.* New York City: Simon & Schuster.

Khan, W. A. (1990). Psychological conditions of personal engagement and disengagement at work. *Academy of Management Journal, 33,* pp. 692-724.

Levinson, H., **Price**, C. R., **Munden**, K. J., & **Solley** C. M. (1962). *Men, management and mental health.* Cambridge, Massachusetts: Harvard University Press.

Macey, W. H., & **Schneider**, B. (2006). Employee experiences and customer satisfaction: Toward a framework for survey design with a focus on service climate. In A.I. Kraut (Ed.), *Getting action from organisational surveys* (pp. 53-75). San Francisco: Jossey-Bass.

MacLeod, D., & **Clarke**, N. (2009). *Engaging for success: Enhancing performance through employee engagement.* Department for Business, Innovation and Skills, London.

Maslach, C., **Schaufeli**, W. B., & **Leitner**, M. P. (2001). Job burnout. *Annual Review of Psychology, 52*, pp. 397-422.

O'Connor, J., & **McDermott**, I. (1997). The art of systems thinking. Thorsons, London

Quinn, R. E., & **McGrath**, M. R. (1985). The transformation of organisational cultures: A competing values perspective. In P. J. Frost, L. F. Moore, M. R. Louise, C. C. Lundberg, & J. Martin (Eds.), *Organisational culture* (315-334). Newbury Park, California: Sage.

Robinson, D., **Perryman**, S., & **Hayday**, S. (2004). *The drivers of employee engagement.* Brighton, U.K.: Institute for Employment Studies.

Saks, A. M. (2006). Antecedents and consequences of employee engagement. *Journal of Managerial Psychology, 21*(7), pp. 600-619

Scholtz, C. (1987). Corporate culture and strategy—the problem of strategic fit. *Long Range Planning, 20*(4), pp.78-87.

Watson Wyatt Worldwide, Work 2000 (2001)

Wellins, R., & **Concelman**, J. (2005). *Creating a culture for engagement.* Workforce Performance Solutions. (www.wpsmag.com). Retrieved July 19, 2005, from www.ddiworld.com/pdf/wps_engagement_ar.pdf

The FIRM™ Communication Management Matrix and the Seven Cs of Change™ are owned by Q⁴ consulting limited.

Useful addresses:

www.q4metrics.com
www.ghost-partnership.com
www.q4consulting.com

ABOUT THE AUTHOR

Alan Crozier is a founding director of The Ghost Partnership and has been managing director of Q⁴ consulting limited since 2002. He has worked in consulting for over 20 years, and spent 13 of those years in senior positions at Mercer and Watson Wyatt.

Alan has served on the Steering Board of the Corporate Identity Group, the Professional Advisory Board of the MSc in Corporate Communication Management at Salford University, and on the accreditation council for the International Association of Business Communicators (IABC). He is a Fellow of the Chartered Management Institute and an Accredited Business Communicator (the professional accreditation of IABC).

Alan has written for professional journals and talked at conferences in Europe and North America. His seminal paper on Employer Branding, "Total Employment Relationship Management" was published by Fairleigh Dickinson University in 1998. He is a contributing author to *The IABC Handbook of Organisational Communication*, published by Jossey Bass, 2006, and *Integrating HR and Marketing Strategies*, published by ICFAI University, July 2006.